Frank Auerbach

Robert Hughes

Frank Auerbach

With 174 illustrations in duotone and 80 in colour

Thames and Hudson

Frontispiece Frank Auerbach, 1989, by Julia Auerbach

The Publishers gratefully acknowledge the assistance given
by the Artist's Agents Marlborough Fine Art (London) Ltd.

Designed by Ruth Rosenberg

Set in Monophoto Poliphilus
Printed and bound in Japan by Dai Nippon

Contents

I

Frank Auerbach's career says little about 'the art world', except that it may not matter much to a real artist's growth.

Auerbach entered art school in 1948, as a teenager. Since then he has done nothing but paint and draw, either from the posed model or from quick landscape scribbles done outside, ten hours a day, seven days a week, in the same studio in north-west London. He has hardly any social life beyond his contacts with a small circle of other artists in London: Leon Kossoff, Francis Bacon, Lucian Freud, R. B. Kitaj. He does not teach. He has travelled very little. To be on any kind of international circuit is and always has been quite alien to Auerbach: the museums he has not been to would include the Prado, the Hermitage, the Uffizi, and all American ones except – during two brief visits to New York in 1969 and 1982 – the Metropolitan, the Frick and the Museum of Modern Art. He has been to Italy twice, the first time for a show of his work in Milan in 1973, the second for his exhibition in the British Pavilion at the 1986 Venice Biennale. The first visit took a week and the second four days, including a trip to Padua to see, for the first time, Giotto's frescoes in the Arena Chapel.

On the other hand, Auerbach's attachment to the National Gallery in London is deep and almost fanatical; throughout the 1950s, 60s and 70s he and his friend Kossoff kept up what struck other artists and students as the quaint habit of going to Trafalgar Square at least once a week to make drawings from certain paintings there. 'Rembrandt in the National Gallery – I went every day, for a long time. I drew from paintings then drew them as if I'd drawn them myself . . . I looked at them again and drew over them. Turner, Tintoretto, Poussin – Tintoretto has tremendous brilliance, tremendous energy . . . Rembrandt and Tintoretto seem to be the polarity of what can be called good painting – the gaiety of Tintoretto, the conscientiousness of Rembrandt, his doggedness.'[1] Such work has always been deeply energizing to Auerbach, as he told the art historian Catherine Lampert, one of his more frequent models: 'My most complimentary and my most typical reaction to a good painting is to want to rush home and do some more work . . . Towards the end of a painting I actually go and draw from pictures more, to remind myself of what quality is and what's actually demanded of paintings. Without these touchstones we'd be floundering. Painting is a cultured activity – it's not like spitting, one can't kid oneself.'[2]

Auerbach's feelings about the museum have nothing to do with the exploitable reverence, the idea of the museum as secular cathedral, that contributed so many grotesqueries to our institutional culture. He treats it as a writer treats a library: as a resource, a 'professional facility'. 'Your correspondents tend to write of paintings as objects of financial value or passive beauty', he protested in a letter to *The Times* in 1971.[3] 'For painters they are source material: they teach and they set standards.' There is perhaps no living artist more wholeheartedly in accord with Cézanne's dictum that 'The path to Nature lies through the Louvre, and to the Louvre through Nature.' Auerbach does not believe that modern art made a radical break with the past. 'From Giotto until now it's one school of art and I don't think that necessarily the most radical twist occurred around 1907. What happened in France around David's time and later, when people suddenly began to invent totally independent languages for noting down what they were doing, showed at least as radical a change. Géricault, Delacroix, Corot, Courbet, Ingres, Daumier – they came up with languages of a hitherto unknown disparity.'[4]

These languages are present to him, as those of his or her medium must be to any serious artist. An interviewer in 1986 who asked Auerbach what artists had influenced him got a Borges-like list of more than fifty names off the top of the head, of whom no more than a third had worked in the twentieth century and only three (Willem de Kooning, Leon Kossoff and Francis Bacon) were alive.[5] With some, one sees the affinity at once. The internal glow that works its way out of Auerbach's heads is partly the result of long meditation on Rembrandt. There is much in common between the overloaded surfaces of early Auerbach and the pelleted, moulded skin of Giacometti's bronzes, which were in turn fed by the harsh impacted blobbiness of Daumier's tiny clay sculptures, *Les Célébrités du Juste-Milieu*; and all three have in common a fiercely sustained remoteness as things-in-the-world, a disdain for the merely expressive. The way a single brushstroke turns, slaps and becomes an autonomous sign for chin or cheek in Auerbach's portraits of J.Y.M. in the 1970s puts one immediately in mind of the radical abbreviations in Manet and, even more, the twisting faces in Goya's 'black paintings'. The geometrical gridding of Auerbach's cityscapes of Camden Town has Mondrian in it, and his landscapes of Primrose Hill pay homage to Constable. But Whistler? Gainsborough? David? Vermeer? In fact, the sign of an educated artist is the ability to get something out of other art that has nothing overtly to do with his or her own: that 'something' is the sense of quality, of eloquence and precision within the matrix of a different style, epoch and idea. The sense of the museum as one's natural ground – not just a warehouse of motifs to be 'appropriated' but rather the house of one's dead peers from whose unenforceable verdict there is no appeal but with whom endless conversation is possible – this has never left Auerbach, as it never left Giacometti; it hovers behind even the most abrupt and ejaculatory of his works. 'When I see the great pictures of the world paraded in my mind's eye', he remarked,

they are great images which don't leak into other images, they are new things. I could name them, or try to name 20 of them – the Kenwood House Rembrandt is pretty close, the Picasso of the pre-Cubist period called *Head (Femme au nez en quart de Brie)* seems to me to be one of them. There's a blue cut-out late Matisse, *Acrobats*. There's the Dürer with the bent nose (*Conrad Vernell*), a Philips Koninck landscape *View in Holland*. One hopes somehow to make something that has a similar degree of individuality, independence, fullness and perpetual motion to these pictures. But actually one hopes, though of course one won't achieve it . . . to surpass them.[6]

II

Exiled to England at the age of eight, orphaned by Hitler soon afterwards, Auerbach is possessed by filiation. He has transposed the wound of parental loss into the realm of art-making, and sighted in with awesome concentration – the attentiveness of instinct, rather than of formal art-historical analysis – on how past art might speak to, and through, images made in the present. We do not choose our parents. Painters are drawn to their ancestors by a homing impulse that works below 'strategy'. In this they are both free and not free. This is not like shopping around for a style to adopt. It is deeper and more compulsive. It is to know one's heritage, its limits, the challenges these present. Each bloodline entails responsibilities. Auerbach's is squarely in the 'great tradition' of figure-painting. He was taught by David Bomberg, who had been the pupil of Sickert, who was the friend and best English interpreter of Degas, whom Ingres begat. He still regards the posed human figure as the ultimate test and unweakening source of a painter's capabilities.

In the 1970s this put him beyond the pale of fashion: a murky 'Jewish expressionist' whose small gnomic renderings of the human figure in terms of abrupt scrawls and pilings of thick pigment were very far from American 'post-painterly' abstraction, let alone the iconic brashness of Pop. He was after heavy, sculptural, tactile form, the exact reverse of the 'optical' colour and agreeable clarity of profile valued in the 60s, from Kenneth Noland to David Hockney. Moreover, Auerbach was not just un-ironical – his painting bluntly rejected the *possibility* of detachment. In the 1960s and through into the 70s irony looked like a fresh posture: a bright, undeceived way of looking at a culture in transition, of feeling out the tingling shudder of reality-loss occasioned by mass electronic media: 'nothing is real / Nothing to get hung about / Strawberry Fields forever'. The ease with which the times rejected internalization did not favour a sympathetic reading of Auerbach's work.

Today, of course, that innocence has gone and is replaced by something worse – a soured relativism, rising from our media-fixated social environment, that in the name of 'irony' derides almost any attempt at deep pictorial authenticity as a trap or an illusion. Irony is merely the condom of our culture, and it does not help much in understanding an artist whose ambition has always pointed to exacerbation, doggedness, courage, rawness and the slow formation of his own values. And 'newness' too: the peculiar freshness of unmediated experience.

The idea of newness has intense significance for Auerbach. But it has nothing to do with that exhausted cultural artefact, the idea of the avant-garde. Auerbach's 'newness' means vitality, the seizure of something real from the world and its coding – however imperfect and approximate – in paint. It does not mean a new twist of syntax. 'There is no syntax in painting. Anything can happen on the canvas and you can't foresee it. Paul Valéry used to say that if the idea of poetry hadn't existed for ever, poetry could not be written now. The whole culture is against it because language is always being worn down and debased. But painting is always a fresh language because we don't use it for anything else. It has no other uses. It isn't mass persuasion.'

Nor is 'newness' a matter of style: 'The idiom is the least important thing. If a painting is good enough the idiom falls away with time, and there's the object, raw and immediate. Think of young Pierre Matisse in *The Piano Lesson*: a horrible, resentful little boy – knowing, precocious, sly. It's all there. Or think of Madame Matisse having tea in the garden, the garden furniture, the ceremony of *thé à l'anglaise*: he couldn't have done it like Monet, because it wouldn't have been real. He had to do it new, and make it real.'

Auerbach's 'newness' is existential, not stylistic. 'I do want them [the works] to be alive, and they don't come alive to me in ways that are full of clichés or if they seem incomplete or not coherent . . . I think the unity in any painter's work arises from the fact that a person, brought to a desperate situation, will behave in a certain way.' Stress produces constants and these constants are the style. 'That's what real style is: it's not donning a mantle or having a programme, it's how one behaves in a crisis.'[7]

Newness rises from repetition. It is the unfamiliar found in the midst of the most familiar sight, like the head of someone you have been painting for twenty years. The element of surprise is 'enormously important to me. To do something predicted doesn't seem to me to be worth doing at all. To do something one hadn't foreseen – by itself – seems to me to be just a gesture, and I can't see how that would be interesting. But to have done something both unforeseen and true to a specific fact seems to me to be very exciting.'

The work is full of observed facts of posture, gesture, expression, stare, the configuration of the head in all its parts, the tenseness or slump of a body, alertness or boredom, light and shadow: the endless drama of the I and the Other. The brush does not so much 'describe' these as go to inquisitorial lengths in finding kinetic and haptic equivalents for them. A dense structure unfolds as you look. The essential subject of the work, however, is not that structure as a given thing, but rather the process of its discovery.

In the mid-50s and through the 60s the English critics Andrew Forge and David Sylvester wrote about Auerbach with insight and enthusiasm, but to most his work seemed ill-synchronized with its times.[8] In the late 60s and early 70s, as he was moving towards real maturity as a painter, his isolation was especially severe; he looked like Pound's M. Verog:

> Out of step with his decade
> Detached from his contemporaries
> Neglected by the young
> Because of these reveries.

Stubbornness exacts its price. In 1986 the critic Stuart Morgan assured the readers of *Vogue* that Auerbach was 'the ultimate pig-headed Englishman', condemned by his own narcissism to do the same thing over and over again.[9] This is a thin, peevish reading, but one can see why such irritations are felt. There are dumb ways of liking any serious painter's work. In Auerbach's case the *idée reçue* is to attach pseudo-moral value to the inordinate thickness of his paint, which is the most obvious feature of his work and threatens it with cliché, as drips do Pollock or dots Seurat. Heavy paint looks *worthy*; it suggests mucky integrity. As Andrew Forge remarked in 1963, apropos of Auerbach's thickest and most heavily trowelled paintings, 'It has been taken . . . rather insultingly, as a sign of his seriousness, as though it proved he tries hard.'[10] Today we know thick paint is as much a code as thin, that neither is more 'sincere' or 'urgent' than the other. Who was in more travail – Ingres weeping with frustration as he struggled to get the thin vellum-like bloom on M. Bertin's sallow cheeks right, or some neo-Expressionist in the 1980s prolifically turning out his signs for extreme insecurity? If the thickness of Auerbach's paint does have expressive value, it must rise from some source other than these conventions of sentiment.

To be seen as a peripheral painter, stubbornly holding ground nobody else much wanted in the 60s and 70s, excluded Auerbach from what people still called the avant-garde. In the process his work survived this glib and superficial idea of the progressive. Modernist 'progress' in art, once an unquestioned faith, seems the merest illusion at the end of the 80s, and there is absolutely no reason to suppose that the 'newness' of a work of art generates any kind of aesthetic value. In our *fin-de-siècle* we realize what harm this fantasy has done: how it abbreviated aesthetic response and created set menus of novelty for cultural tourists: above all, how it replaced the organic complexities of a serious artist's relation to the past with a shallow puppet-show in which hostility to the ancestors mingles with bombastic claims of equality to them:

> It takes exceptional historical imagination to reconstruct the boldness and independence of mind of (say) Newton in the act of radically re-writing the laws of nature. In Masaccio, in Michelangelo, in Velázquez or Cézanne the personal heroism and genius is woven into the fabric of the work – also, in the history of art, it becomes clear that as we gain one insight and skill we lose another – we cannot now paint like Bruegel since we do not have the tension of discovery which produce[d] his work. Otherwise – I feel quite close to scientists . . . the way Kepler arrived at true discoveries on false premises simply by obsessively going over his data seems familiar.[11]

Art is not like science, though scientific experiment has some of the character of art. Science progresses, art does not. Any third-year medical sudent knows more about the fabric of the human body than Vesalius, but no one alive today can draw as well as Rubens. In art there are no 'advances', only alterations of meaning, fluctuations of intensity and quality. The modernist sense of cultural time, fixed on the dictatorial 'possibilities' of the historicist moment, is a lie. It has distorted our sense of relation to the living body of art, most of which lies in the past and none in the future, to an absurd degree.

And so in cultural compressors like London or, especially, like New York in the late twentieth century, obsessed with rapid stylistic turnover (which is what capitalism, in its need to encourage novelty and diversity, made of avant-gardism), Auerbach does indeed look odd. His project as an artist has to do with arresting (just for himself, and for one viewer at a time) the sense of leakage between images that, under the pressure of other media, has been set up as a 'post-modernist' value. And seeing one thing well, clearly and 'raw' (a favourite adjective with Auerbach), especially in a way that has no relation to photography and in fact defies everything implied by the rapid glance of pattern-recognition we bestow on media images, means seeing it over and over again. 'I'm hoping to make a new thing', he once remarked, 'that remains in the mind like a new species of living thing . . . The only way I know how . . . to try and do it, is to start with something I know specifically, so that I have something to cling to beyond aesthetic feelings and my knowledge of other paintings. Ideally one should have more material than one can possibly cope with.'[12] But the 'material' must be impacted into one thing at a time.

III

Perhaps one should begin where the paintings do, in Frank Auerbach's studio, a brown cave in north-west London where he has worked for more than thirty years.

It is one of a line of three studios in an alley that runs off a street in Camden Town, a rootedly lower-middle-class area between Mornington Crescent and the park of Primrose Hill. They were built around 1900, with high north-facing windows. Auerbach 'inherited' his from Kossoff, in 1954; before Kossoff, it had been used by photographers and, earlier, by the painter Frances Hodgkins. The emblematic artist of Camden Town, up to that time, had of course been Walter Richard Sickert (1860–1942), who kept a studio a couple of hundred yards away at 6 Mornington Crescent – a narrow three-storey terrace house whose stucco facade is as dingy today as it probably was then. The flavour of Camden Town recalls a fact of Sickert's work which applies to Auerbach's today – its attachment to the common-and-garden, to the compost of life as it is lived.

You enter the alley through a wicket gate, set between a liver-brick Victorian semi-detached villa on the left and on the right a decayed block of 60s maisonettes. A roughly lettered sign says TO THE STUDIOS. Auerbach's door opens on a scene of dinginess and clutter. The studio is actually a generous-sized room, but it seems constricted at first, all peeling surfaces, blistered paint, spalling plaster, mounds and craters of paint, piles of newspapers and books crammed into rickety shelves, a mirror so frosted with dust that movements reflected inside it are barely decipherable. It is a midden-heap. Because Auerbach paints thick and scrapes off all the time, the floor is encrusted with a deposit of dried paint so deep that it slopes upwards several inches, from the wall to the easel. One walks, gingerly, on the remains of innumerable pictures. Where he sets his drawing easel this lava is black from accumulated charcoal dust. 'I changed the lino three times', Auerbach says. 'The last time quite recently, less than ten years ago. If I didn't, the paint would be up to here.' He gestures at thigh-height. And then, a few days later: 'Leonardo said painting is better than sculpture because painters kept clean. How wrong he was!'

The walls are brown, mottled with damp-borne salts. The high north window has not been cleaned in years. It does admit light: on fine May days a tender Rembrandtian gloom, in February a grim Dickensian one. The only colour is the paint itself – the canvas on the easel, and two palettes. The first of these is a slab, perhaps wood, perhaps stone, turgid with pigment inches thick. The second is an extraordinary object, the fossil of a wooden box upended, so that its midway partition acts as a shelf. Warm colours are mixed on the top of the box, cool ones on the shelf. Years of use have turned it into a block of pigment, its sides encrusted with glistening cakes and stalactites of the same magma that encrusts the floor. One side of the box is partly worn through by the slapping of Auerbach's brushes. The darkness and dirt of the studio are only relieved by the gleam of the paint: a bright epiphany of raw material, cadmium red, cadmium yellow, flake white, pure and buttery in their tins.

Images are pinned on the window wall and above the sink: a photo of Rembrandt's patriarchal head of Jakob Trip and another of Saskia; a small self-portrait by Auerbach's early friend and dealer Helen Lessore, a reproduction of Lucian Freud's head of Auerbach himself, the forehead bulging from the surface with tremendous, knotted plasticity; a drawing by Dürer of Conrat Verkell's head seen from below, the features gnarled and squeezed like the flesh structure in one of Auerbach's portraits; souvenirs of the work of friends (Bacon, Kossoff, Kitaj) and of dead masters. They are all emblems and have been there for years, browned and cockled, like votives of legs and livers hanging in a Greek shrine. A string runs from above the sink to below the window, carrying a line of yellowed sheets of newspaper, years old. Auerbach hangs his underpants on it to dry. New newspapers will not do, because their ink leaches into the cotton. Paper towels will not do, because (one supposes) they would be too white. Like one of Beckett's paralysed heroes, like Sterne's father in *Tristram Shandy*, who put up with a squeaking door all his life because he could not summon up the decision to apply a few drops of oil to the hinges, Auerbach is inured to his own domestic irritants. They are part of the solemn game of stasis.

The essence of this place is that things do not change in it, except that dust accumulates, waste pigment slowly builds its reef on the floor, the light fluctuates, models (as few as possible, and nearly always the same ones, because Auerbach does not do commissions and not many people can endure the arduous business of posing for him) arrive, sit for three hours, and go; paintings and drawings are finished and are taken away. The studio is the antitype of the Matissean ideal. But it offers the painter a certain stability, a guarantee of changelessness, as Nice did Matisse. 'In order to paint my pictures', Matisse remarked, 'I need to remain for several days in the same state of mind, and I do not find this in any atmosphere but that of the Cote d'Azur.' So with Auerbach and his studio. It is a troglodyte's den of internalization, the refuge in which the artist becomes unavailable, digging back into the solitary indurated habits without which nothing can be imagined, made or fully seen. There is no television set – 'a barbarous invention' – and, of course, no telephone.

The position of each easel is fixed. The wooden chair in which the sitter poses is also fixed, with a white circle drawn on the floor around each leg. To the left of the chair is a pedestal paraffin-heater, unlit, on which the sitter balances a cup of strong coffee and an ashtray. To the right is another heater, mercifully red-hot, with another locating circle of white paint drawn around its base. You know you may not move it, and do not try to. You roast on one side and freeze on the other. The distance between Auerbach's surface and the sitter's face is always the same. The sitter has only one way to sit: facing the easel, staring back at the stare. Whatever happens to left or right is not part of a room; it is just 'space'. The purple cover on the studio bed has its own role in the light, as the sitter will find when, coming in from the underground station at 7.30 one winter morning, he throws his *Times* on it; after twenty minutes' work Auerbach screws up his face and complains about the nagging white light reflected from the paper. This morning in February 1986 there are other irritations. The outside lavatory has frozen and the ice in the bowl has to be broken with jabs of a broom-handle. Inside the studio, a plastic jug of turps has cracked in the cold and flooded the floor under the sink.

The work of drawing begins. Auerbach has a sheet of paper, or rather two sheets glued together, ready on the easel. The paper is a stout rag, almost as thick as elephant hide, resistant to the incessant rubbing-out that will go on for days and weeks. As he scribbles and saws at the paper, the sticks of willow charcoal snap; they make cracking sounds like a tooth breaking on a bone. When he scrubs the paper with a rag clouds of black dust fly. An hour into the session the sitter blows his nose and finds his snot is black. The studio is like a colliery; the drawing easel is black and exquisitely glossy from years of carbon dust mixed with hand-grease. Auerbach works on the balls of his feet, balanced like a welterweight boxer, darting in and out. Sometimes he and the sitter talk about painting, and poetry. He recites from memory long runs of Yeats, George Barker and Auden. Asked if he ever works to music, he answers with a curious vehemence: 'Oh, no, never! I like silence! I think I must be completely unmusical. I can't remember phrases; that makes me useless in a concert-hall. If you're to enjoy music I suppose you have to remember something of what went before in order to grasp what you're hearing at the moment – and I can't. That rubbish of Pater's! It is *absolutely* untrue that art aspires to the condition of music. Painting never wants to be like music. It is best when it is *least* like music: fixed, concrete, immediate and resistant to time.' Then he shuts up and goes into high gear, working with redoubled concentration, cocking his head at the sitter and grimacing. He hisses and puffs. He darts back to consult the reflection of the drawing in a mirror on the wall; the sitter sees Auerbach's peering reflection, the chin and cheeks smudged with black. Sometimes his mouth broadens into a rictus of anxiety, very much like a Japanese armour-mask. He talks to himself. 'Now what feels specially untrue?' 'Yes, yes.' 'That's it.' 'Come on, come *on*!' And a long-drawn-out, morose 'No-o-o.' Now and again he fumbles out a book from the nearby shelf, opens it to a reproduction – Giacometti's *Woman with her Throat Cut*, Cézanne's *Self-portait with Cap*, 1873–75, from the Hermitage, Vermeer's young turbaned girl – and lays it on the

1 Portrait of Robert Hughes 1986

floor where he can see it, 'to have something good to look at', a purpose not kind to the sitter's vanity until one understands that Auerbach is hoping for osmosis. By the end of the day the drawing is some kind of a likeness, though not a flattering one: a blackened Irishman with a squashed nose and a thick, swinging chop of shadow under his right cheekbone. Through the next twelve sittings, spaced over not quite four weeks, this creature will mutate, becoming dense and troll-like one day and dissolving in *furioso* passages of hatching the next; lost in thought in one version, belligerently staring in another, eye contact almost obliterated in a third as the mass of the face is lost in a welter of hooking lines (the hair) and zigzag white scribbles of the eraser (a twisting in the space behind the head). In the end, the likeness is retrieved, but as a ghost, the colour of very tarnished silver.

IV

Frank Helmut Auerbach was born in Germany to Jewish parents in 1931. His mother, Charlotte Nora Borchardt, was Lithuanian – a former art student, who after a brief and unhappy previous marriage had met and married Max Auerbach, a well-to-do patent lawyer whose practice lay in Berlin. Law was the profession of the whole Auerbach clan; out of a swarm of five uncles, four were lawyers.

Auerbach remembers few details of his Berlin infancy and childhood. His main memory is of a pall of parental strain and worry that seemed to lie across everything he did. His parents were frightened both as bourgeois and as Jews, for themselves and for their son. The year Frank Auerbach was born was also the year the Austrian Credit-Anstalt Bank collapsed, sending fiscal shudders through central Europe; within months the closure of the German Danatbank had led to the temporary shutdown of the whole German banking system. The SA brownshirts were marching in the Berlin streets when Auerbach was learning to toddle. When he was nearly two, Hitler became Chancellor and, through an Enabling Law, dictator of Germany; the boycott of Jews began, and the first concentration camps were set up. Through folksong and beerhall, the incantatory screaming of loudspeakers and the crunch of boots on broken glass, the fate of European Jewry began to move towards its administrative climax. People like Auerbach's parents, the liberal, educated German Jews of the professional classes, men and women in whose family traditions *stetl* and pogrom were vague memories at most, could not imagine the Final Solution; it still lay incubating, like a dragon's egg, in the minds of Hitler and Himmler. But the Auerbachs lived in growing anxiety, like the parents of another Berlin Jew who years later was to become one of their son's few intimates in London, the painter Lucian Freud. The fear of giving offence to the majority culture of German gentiles was bred into any assimilated, middle-class Jewish boy in Berlin, to a degree inconceivable in a Polish *stetl*. It seems to have hung like a pall over the Auerbachs' domestic life, which was not altogether happy in any case. With their son it came out in what Auerbach remembers as 'frantic coddling'. 'I remember velvet knickerbocker suits and no freedom. I couldn't run in the park near the house. I couldn't step outside the door on my own, of course; and my mother would begin to worry if my father was half an hour late home.' The little boy could not make sense of this. He accepted the protection he needed but balked at the rest, translating it, in adulthood, into 'a profound impatience with the self-protective life of the bourgeoisie.'

By 1937 it was clear that the six-year-old boy was going to be in real danger if he stayed in Germany. But his father would not go; presumably, like many other Jews, he hoped that Nazism would soften, that its racial policy would be diluted by cultural and economic necessity, and that resolute adults might still breathe the air that would choke a little boy. Auerbach was saved by chance and luck. In 1937 the partner of one of his lawyer uncles had gone to Italy and in Tuscany he met the writer Iris Origo, the future author of *The Merchant of Prato*, her now-classic study of the *quattrocento* Florentine wool trade. Princess Origo had begun to worry about the impending fate of Jewish children in the Reich and she decided to do something practical about it, however small: better one act of real charity than any amount of talk. She agreed to put up the money for the keep and education of six boys and girls if they were sent to safe haven in an English school. None of the children were personally known to her. One was Auerbach. It took time to make the arrangements; more time, almost, than the family had. In the early spring of 1939 the Auerbachs packed their son's bag, took the train to Hamburg and put him on a ship to England. It sailed on 4 April, just before his eighth birthday.

Auerbach never saw his parents again. Over the next three years, a few Red Cross letters – postcard messages restricted to twenty-five words, which gave no real news except the indication that Max and Charlotte Auerbach were still alive – found their way to him in England. But after 1942 there was nothing. The ovens had swallowed them. Soon after the end of the War, one of Auerbach's friends recalls, he received a package containing some of his father's effects, including a gold watch. He took it to a jeweller's, sold it and used the money to buy another watch. Years would pass before he would speak of his parents to anyone.

Can one speculate about how, if at all, this catastrophic loss might have borne on Auerbach's work? 'It is, or it is not, according to the nature of men', wrote Thomas de Quincey, parentless himself, 'an advantage to be orphaned at an early age.' Every year, millions of children are torn from parental security, cast bereaved into the world, orphaned for reasons they cannot grasp and will unconsciously misinterpret for the rest of their lives; among them, some tiny fraction of a percentage grow up to be painters or sculptors; the idea that there is some necessary or predictable connection between the loss of one's parents and the shaped concerns of one's work as an adult (as though a common trauma inscribed itself in a common style) is clearly absurd. That Auerbach in boyhood must have instinctively construed his own exile and his parents' death as their abandonment of him is likely, indeed certain; from the watch story, one can deduce an unassuagable, yearning aggression against the lost father. And just as Auerbach's early paintings seem, at root, to be attempts to contact his own infancy and put himself, through the metaphor of paint as a primal substance – the touch that precedes sight – once again in contact with the lost body of his mother, so the images in the final state of certain drawings, these blackened wraiths of ash, rendered into weightlessness over the long course of construction and disembodiment, carry an inescapable freight of pain: these images conjured out of the dust of burnt wood might come from inside the chimney, from within the final and unappeasable loss of her body.

Early parental loss can be the most powerful of creative goads. We patch together structures, solid or rickety, to fill the emotional void, and invest them with a degree of healing power. The future artist or intellectual, having suffered as a child the lovelessness, abandonment and terror of one's own death that are the inseparable consequences of the death of one's parents, may indeed find creative risk more tolerable because of the feeling of power and self-sufficiency that its successful outcome gives: an early loss may (or as de Quincey reminds us, may not) favour later leaps in the dark. At the same time the hunger for security may inscribe itself in the child's adult habits, and this may perhaps cast some light on Auerbach's singularly fixed and stable rituals: the daily routine of work, work and more work, early morning to dusk; the unchanging studio, embalmed in waste paint, guarded by scraps and emblems; the long construction and daily erasure and unpicking of the image, like Penelope's weaving; the doggedness of repeated attack on a familiar motif which is the peculiar mark of Auerbach's temperament. The family intimacy denied to him in boyhood is summoned and re-enacted in his work, in his hourly transactions with the object of scrutiny. 'To paint the same head over and over', he will say, 'leads you to its unfamiliarity; eventually you get near the raw truth about it, *just as people only blurt out the raw truth in the middle of a family quarrel.*' In a more general way, Auerbach's work is quite free of the displaced Oedipal struggle – the desire to murder the paternal tradition, whether framed in Futurist manifestos or *soixante-huitard* calls to radical cultural renewal – which was such a feature of avant-garde mythology in his youth. He derides 'artists who produce a smooth series of radical-looking changes but no upheaval at all'. Auerbach would seek forms from which a full sense of 'reality' could be unpacked – the structure, weight, density, malleability and resistance of the object, the stare of a head in the studio, the sag and sheen of a nude's belly, the bustling sky over a zigzag tree in Primrose Hill. But at the same time, every one of his paintings, the failures as well as the successes, is imprinted with the desire to engage on levels deeper than mere quotation with the great tradition of Western figurative art, a tradition mangled and weakened almost beyond recognition in the last half of the twentieth century. He is, in short, a conservative artist. The tension between radical will and conservatism gives Auerbach's work, as it gave Giacometti's, much of its peculiar intensity. It may well be that the emotional roots of his convictions about the nurturing past that pervade Auerbach's art wind back, however tenuously, to the eight-year-old boy who came down the gangway of the ship from Hamburg on 7 April, 1939 and found himself with two newly made shipboard friends and their nursemaid on the dock at Southampton, clutching a suitcase, ready to start learning in a strange country.

V

Bunce Court, at Lenham near Faversham in Kent, was one of England's more remarkable experiments in 'progressive' education: an eccentric, idealistic place conceived and run by Anna Essinger, a German Jewish Quaker. 'Tanta Anna', as she was nicknamed in later life, had gone to study in America just before World War I. She stayed with Quaker friends in Philadelphia and was struck by the amount of practical influence the Society of Friends (which was hardly more than a fringe sect in Germany) had gained in America. When she got back to Germany after the Armistice she applied herself, in the vortex of Weimar inflation, to the management of American Quaker funds for the relief of German children; suddenly, as she later put it, she was responsible for 250,000 kids without knowing a single one of them. This seemed unduly abstract to Anna Essinger, so she started a private school, the Landschulheim at Herrlingen in southern Germany, not far from Ulm. She ran it for the better part of a decade, but in 1932 this redoubtable woman realized that its days – and those of more than half its pupils, the Jewish ones – were numbered. She decided to get them to safety in England, where she would start a new school for them. She beseeched and badgered the parents to part with their children; not all of them would, since in 1933 many Jews still hoped Hitler could be reasoned with. But some did give in to Essinger's entreaties, and towards the end of 1933 she took ship for England with a sizeable brood. With the help of some English Jews, in particular the Left Book Club publisher Victor Gollancz, she was able to buy the rambling, unkempt country house Bunce Court and on a tiny budget convert it into what seemed, to the conventional wisdom of English pedagogy fifty years ago, a bizarre experiment: a co-educational boarding school for refugees run, without corporal punishment, along the lines of liberal arts, plain living and high thinking.

When Frank Auerbach arrived clutching his suitcase, it cheered him to see 'wild, long-haired, scruffy kids running everywhere'. Clearly, the velvet knickerbockers and wringing hands were in the past; and the miseries of his homesickness were somewhat eased when he found that so many of the pupils were German.

The school and its pupils were evacuated to Shropshire from 1940 to 1945, so that Auerbach grew up in the green depths of the English countryside, far from the waves of Luftwaffe bombers that were pulverizing London. It is not easy to evoke what it was like for a young German Jew, living in the island haven of England during the Blitz, feeling sheltered from the Germans and yet close to them, with the most precarious of divisions – a small moat, the English Channel – between security and death. It raised in many of them (and Auerbach was no exception) an extreme sense of gratitude, more vivid than any American equivalent. Beyond the Channel, the nightmare; one sees the root of Auerbach's passionate Englishness, and his lifelong aversion to foreign travel.

Bunce Court gave him a sense of place, and a stimulating and venturesome (if erratic) education. The school was long on idealism and short of money, desperately so much of the time. Its English pupils, by his recollection, ran to type: they tended to be the offspring of divorced left-wing parents. Its intellectual background was part

Quaker and part Fabian Socialist, emphasizing communal values and plain living; the refectory tables carried pewter jugs of water, and before each meal the children and teachers were expected to join hands in wordless grace, not formal prayer. 'There was a strong puritan atmosphere, a sense of prissiness about the place. It had considerable cultural snobbery, and gave us the sense of being trained as members of an intellectual élite. The idea that anyone would go on to make money in later life was simply not considered.' 'Streaming' was ignored there, and future scholastic achievement regarded almost as a byproduct. According to Michael Roemer, the film-maker who attended Bunce Court a class ahead of Auerbach, the school was 'very old-style Jewish, in the sense that it placed great importance on the sense of community, on being a good person . . . it had quite a strong kibbutz ethic, or to be exact one which I would be reminded of years later when I first visited Israel . . . its emphasis on the community as family, its sexual restrictiveness. . . . There was a very potent force there, and mostly it emanated from women like "Tanta Anna" and Hannah Bergas. The men were satellites.'[13] (Women far outnumber men among Auerbach's subjects, although David Landau, a friend, has been sitting to him once a week since 1983.) However, Bunce Court's main gift to Auerbach was even more basic than this. It restored his psychic balance by giving him a new family which was, in the main, composed and happy.

Wartime conditions, quite apart from Tanta Anna's own convictions, had ensured Bunce Court's Socialist leanings. Its teachers were either German–Austrian refugees or English conscientious objectors – the school's tight budget could not attract experienced teachers above military age. Most of the non-teaching staff were émigrés. The gardener was a former pupil of the pianist Artur Schnabel. The school boiler-room was stoked by Wilhelm Marckwald, whom Auerbach remembers as 'a theatrical genius of sorts'; a disciple of the German *dramaturg* Leopold Jessner, he had directed the Frankfurt Town Theatre at the precocious age of twenty-three and later gone to Barcelona to make plays and propaganda films for the Spanish Republicans. 'He drilled us. One would spend a whole afternoon working on a short speech. Under Marckwald, the school plays at Bunce Court weren't really school plays at all: they were professional theatre created by a thwarted perfectionist, who had to use the only material he had, wartime ersatz stuff – namely, the talents of children.' Roemer remembers this differently. Marckwald, by his recollection, felt nothing 'ersatz' about his work with schoolchildren: he was a brilliantly creative teacher who tried to engage whomever he was working with as fully as possible, and he thought Auerbach, with time and training, could become a serious actor. 'Marckwald told me years later', says Roemer, 'that Frank's performance as "Everyman" was the most extraordinary thing he had seen at Bunce Court. I can't imagine how a child can be "extraordinary" in that part, but Marckwald was no fool, and if he said that it's probably true.'

Auerbach was a natural mimic – his impersonations of cultural poohbahs are still devastating – but it was through Marckwald's training that his rote verbal memory grew to match his near-archival recollection of painted and plastic form: he can still recite by heart the poetry that most seized his imagination as a young man – Auden, Eliot, Keats, Blake, Donne, Yeats and even lesser-known English writers like George

Barker. Marckwald's professionalism, however disproportionate it may have been to schoolboy theatre, was the first example of obsessive dedication to an art through arduous rehearsal that Auerbach had seen, and it made its mark on him.

Bunce Court offered no art training, apart from the sporadic appearance of 'a curious pipe-smoking woman who acted as housekeeper and drawing teacher'. Nevertheless he drew with enthusiasm and was able to get hold of reproductions of modern art – mostly by Edward Burra and Paul Klee – which he pinned up on the wooden walls of his cubicle. He read R. H. Wilenski's *Modern French Painters*. When he was fifteen he produced a small crisis in school discipline by covering a wall with faces drawn in chalk. 'How was a good Quaker to punish me for such an act of vandalism? I had to rub everything out with an indiarubber, which took ages. Then I had to go into town three miles away and help the butcher, whose van had broken down, to carry the meat for 120 people to school – about forty pounds of it, at wartime rationing rates.'

Auerbach came out of Bunce Court and up to London in 1947 with no very strong feeling of vocation: a sixteen-year-old war orphan, not quite adrift in the postwar city. His parents were dead but a number of Auerbach relatives had settled in London either before or immediately after the War.

Some of the guidance Auerbach needed came from his cousins Gerd and Gerda Boehm, and there was some moral support from an uncle, Jakob Auerbach, who had spent the War in hiding in Holland and come to London after 1946. These relatives, together with a maternal uncle, Hans Borchardt, who lived in Buenos Aires, made up an allowance of four pounds ten shillings a week (not a difficult amount for a young man to live on in London in the late 40s) for the first year or two; Auerbach could pay his share of the rent on a room at 19 Pond Street, which he shared with a musician friend, Rainer Schuelein. He did not feel at ease with these older relatives: 'I saw them very infrequently and didn't really tell them much about what I was doing. I wasn't really under *any* guidance, except that of my past upbringing at Bunce Court.'

Marckwald had given him the idea of going into theatre, and he gravitated towards a left-wing drama group in Kensington, the Unity Theatre. It had strong connections with Bunce Court; one of its members was Herman Essinger, nephew of Tanta Anna, and another was Auerbach's school friend Frank Marcus, future author of *The Killing of Sister George* and other works of black absurdist comedy. Auerbach wanted to do sets and designed one for *The Servant of Two Masters* by Goldoni; he also had an idea – which distantly foreshadowed, perhaps, the claustrophobic fullness of his early pictures, so packed with paint – for an odd kind of *Hamlet*, a *Hamlet* that would lay more visual stress on the labyrinth of court life than on the windy open ramparts of Elsinore: 'a crowded *Hamlet*, with lots of small rooms on the stage, a sort of rabbit-warren.' Auerbach acted, designed and learned a little about lighting.

And although he could not afford tickets to West End theatres, he often went to music-halls. The English music-hall, now an extinct form, fascinated him.

He became a fan in its last years, after World War II; he was seventeen when he first went to the old Metropolitan Theatre in the Edgware Road. At that time some of the great men of the Edwardian music-hall were still on the boards; he saw George Robey, an octogenarian still chanting and dancing and telling 'pretty filthy' anatomical jokes.

His favourites are now mostly forgotten, like Max Miller, a comedian who spouted tit-and-bum patter whilst ramping about the stage in cretonne knickerbockers. 'He could command a full house anywhere south of Birmingham. He was choleric and very mean, like W. C. Fields, and he'd never pay for a drink. He made £900 a week, an immense fortune in those days, and was said to have died leaving secret safe-deposit accounts all over England. I used to admire him – going out alone in front of a hostile crowd, not disguising his partial contempt for the audience, and beating them every time.'

Auerbach was enthralled by the way these old pros would over-rehearse: 'Wearing the resistance of their medium down, like drawing, in a way; that was grist to my mill.'

He identified with their doggedness, the circumscribed forms of their work and the inventions they could embroider over a fixed stereotype. All that chimed with his own temperament, with its attachment to familiar objects of obsessive scrutiny, its search for the raw in the midst of the quotidian. 'I loved to see them working. If people ever assume that ordinary people are unsophisticated they should think of the subtlety, the risk, of music-hall. That's why I dislike the idea of "art for the people" – what people like is *great art!*' In a Shakespearean performance, he argues, 'there is always a certain amount of guaranteed support. The text has authority – a "classic", an historical institution in its own right. The ensemble actors support one another. The status of the whole thing prepares you to assent. But the music-hall comedian has to win from scratch. Think of Tommy Cooper: a large, loud, solitary man in a fez, larger than life, doing failed conjuring tricks before a pitiless audience and regarding his own incompetence, which was feigned, with tolerant stoicism. He wasn't a "great actor". But he was an epitome of risk, courage and dominance.' Such people gave flesh to the ideal of artistic integrity that was slowly beginning to form in young Auerbach's mind.

Auerbach had come out of Bunce Court with his Higher School Certificate but he did not have the certificate in Latin that would have put him in the running for a university scholarship. In any case, he leaned towards art school. His 'consortium of relatives' passed round the hat and assembled not quite enough money between them to pay his tuition. He still needed an art-school scholarship. Bunce Court was 'so innocent, so isolated, that no on had made the slightest effort to get me into an art school', and the only place that would accept him as a temporary student was an arts-and-crafts school called the Hampstead Garden Suburb Institute, which offered some amateurish courses in drawing, illustration and sculpture. Its one strength was its calligraphy lessons, given by its principal, Mr Oliver, a professional calligrapher who had done the lettering on the memorial Stalingrad Sword and now employed his students as apprentices – there being, in postwar England, a heavy demand for blackletter and italic lettering in memorial books of the war-dead. Auerbach had no talent for this. 'I was far too clumsy. I think [the teachers] regarded me as rough, foreign, incompetent and hopeless. I was like a fish out of water.'

Luckily, soon after enrolling at the Institute he got to know a teacher at the St Martin's School of Art, Archibald Ziegler, whose wife had taught at Bunce Court and had some faith in young Auerbach's talents. Ziegler sent him to the principal of St Martin's and Auerbach was accepted as a first-year student for the term starting in September 1948. This left him to fill in two terms elsewhere. He was still a schoolboy, entitled to free bus fares, free milk and a sixpenny lunch allowance. Living on this, he traipsed around the art schools of London with his portfolio of drawings and, in January 1948, was accepted as a temporary student at the Borough Polytechnic, a school south of the Thames near the Elephant and Castle.

The Borough Polytechnic once had some claim to be the most 'advanced' school of painting in London, which was not saying very much: just before World War I it had an experimental moment, under the influence of Roger Fry, who in 1911 with the help of some other English post-Impressionists (including Duncan Grant and Frederick Etchells) decorated its student dining-room. But by the 40s even that genteel claim to modernist credentials had long departed. In the main, it was a commercial art school, and quite a good one; several of the best poster designers in England, such as Thomas Eckersley, taught there. (They had to, to make a living; 'design' was not yet the status career it would become in the 60s.) 'I thought I might be a commercial artist — something to justify myself to my relatives, who were paying for my keep.' The Borough offered courses in engineering and bakery as well as art. It was run by a Mr Patrick, a cake designer whose masterwork had been a tower of a wedding-cake ordered by Buckingham Palace for the marriage of Princess Elizabeth and Prince Philip in November 1947; when Auerbach timidly entered this amiable man's office, the first thing he saw on the wall was a rendered drawing for it, plan, side elevation and exploded section of its internal bracing.

The second object that caught his eye in Mr Patrick's office was a watercolour painted in the 1920s by a teacher at the Borough, David Bomberg.

VI

At the time Auerbach came under his tutelage, Bomberg was fifty-seven, a misfit, and a failure. People thought of him, if at all, as a queer minor fish whose shifts of style – from the abstract puppet figures of his Vorticist years, through the scrupulously rendered *vedute* he made in Palestine in the early 20s and on to the broad landscapes he painted at Cuenca and La Ronda in Spain in the 30s – betokened failures of pictorial nerve. This reputation sprang from the way his work changed after World War I, and it was to dog him for the rest of his life.

David Bomberg (1890–1957) was born in a Birmingham slum and raised in the East End of London. His parents were not strictly Orthodox; in defiance of the Mosaic law against making graven images, his mother Rebecca nurtured his talents as an artist and his father (a raging man prone to depression, as the son would become) did not discourage him. But there was always a *mezuzah* on Abraham Bomberg's door, and his son inherited a hot irascible pride in his Jewish origins and traditions. Bomberg went to art school – evening classes at the Westminster School of Art, where his drawing teacher was Sickert. In 1907 John Singer Sargent, the Van Dyck of Edwardian capitalism, took the seventeen-year-old boy under his wing and got him into the Slade School.

Bomberg came to the Slade filled with self-critical determination to master the most exacting skills of drawing and figure-composition. These never left him, and they gave his transition to a modernist idiom its authenticity. Later he would burn most of his student work, keeping only the drawings that recorded his passage towards Vorticism. But one cannot see Bomberg's radicality and not see how embedded it was in the 'academic' drawing which late modernist art teaching, to its detriment, would jettison half a century later.

To simplify the world, to reduce it to the kind of pared-down signs for body and space that Bomberg would produce in his large Vorticist compositions of 1913 – *The Mud Bath*, *In the Hold* – one must first master it in detail. This passage from detailed scrutiny to abstraction and reduction, whose purpose was to condense and strengthen the visual rhythms that lie muffled in the tangle of objects we see, was one aspect (though only one) of the way of dealing with Nature which Bomberg would later try to transmit to his students, including Auerbach, under the guise of 'The spirit in the mass' – a phrase which had the deepest significance for Bomberg himself, ramified through forty years of work, but which was fated like Hans Hofmann's 'push-pull' to become a catchword. If ever a modernist idiom was hard-won, it was the crowded, canted space, filled with stick-and-block figures ecstatically struggling free from the earth, that Bomberg painted in *The Vision of Ezekiel*, 1912, to illustrate the prophet's foretelling of the restoration of Israel:

Son of Man, these bones are the whole house of Israel: behold, they say, Our bones are dried, and our hope is lost: we are cut off for our parts. . . . And ye shall know that I am the Lord, when I have opened your graves, O my people, and brought you up out of your graves, and shall put my spirit in you, and ye shall live, and I shall place you in your own land . . .

Bomberg's Jewishness was, to put it mildly, at least as important to him as his attachment to the cultural ideas of the modernist circle through which he moved as a youthful prodigy in pre-war London, Wyndham Lewis, T. E. Hulme and the Vorticists. The former lay deep in his frame, the latter did not; and the War would split them asunder.

Until he was sent to the trenches early in 1916, Bomberg had embraced the rhetoric of Vorticism. Art should be hard, stripped, angular, direct; it should praise a 'new age' whose presiding metaphor was the Machine. 'I completely abandon *Naturalism* and Tradition', Bomberg had jotted in his notes for a preface to his July 1914 exhibition at the Chenil Gallery in London; 'where I use Naturalistic Form, I have stripped it of irrelevant matter . . . I look upon *Nature*, while I live in a *steel city*.' It was easy to love the Machine in peacetime, but World War I – the first war in history to industrialize mass death – reduced machine-worship to Utopian babble. Here, written in bogs of decaying flesh, was the truth about man and machine. Nobody in England had imagined this truth in 1915.

In the trenches, Bomberg went through spiritual crisis and nervous breakdown. Close to the edge of suicide, he shot himself in the foot – an offence punishable by firing-squad. Luckily, military justice spared him. After the Armistice he could never return to the naive optimism about the Machine and the robotic Cubist body that had infused his early work of 1913. And if rejecting that meant jettisoning 'mainstream' modernism, so be it. 'We have no need to dwell on the material significance of man's achievement', he wrote later, 'but with the approach of the scientific mechanization and the submerging of individuals we have urgent need of the affirmation of his spiritual significance and his individuality.'[14]

Thus, in his early thirties, Bomberg was drawn back to a close study of nature. Other avant-garde artists (Picasso, Morandi, Nevinson, Derain) felt such 'conservative' impulses after the war but Bomberg took them to extremes and set forth to make scrupulously exact landscape paintings, every rock, bush and wall in place, in Palestine. Thus he hoped to reclaim a sense of the world's wholeness – of order and purpose within reality – shattered by the chaos of war.

Perhaps, as Peter Fuller has suggested, there was a deeper motive in Bomberg's choice of the Holy Land as subject.[15] It was more than an aesthetic choice: the archetypal domain of the Jews (though the state of Israel did not exist and Bomberg in any case had no sympathy with Zionism) would be his landscape of consolation.

But be that as it may, Bomberg's 'apostasy' from modernism in the 20s was no failure of nerve, but an act of some courage, a *gran rifiuto*. By it, he denied himself a place in the avant-garde whilst rejecting the tepid conventions of most English figurative painting. What struck his critics as vacillation came from an exacerbated sense of moral responsibility about what an artist might, and might not, affirm. The strengths of Bomberg's work and the miseries of his life stemmed from it. To understand Auerbach's convictions one must look to Bomberg, his exemplar: much of the younger man – his empiricism, his scorn for modernist conventions, his impatience with theory and ideology, his reverence for the past and his determination to paint as though there were no breach between it and the present – was there in the older.

In postwar London Bomberg's career flopped. For the last fourteen years of his life no gallery would touch his work. If he was his own worst enemy, it was only because no one thought him worth opposing. But in the summer of 1945 he did obtain a post, meagre though it was, teaching a part-time life class at the Borough Polytechnic. Very occasionally, the work of some part of a generation will be nurtured by one charismatic teacher acting on a handful of gifted students. So with Hans Hofmann in New York in the 40s. So, too, with Bomberg at this minor school in London, whose students included Auerbach and later Kossoff.

Bomberg's attitude to teaching was not in the least casual. Not for him the common assumption that one taught merely to get a living, that teaching was something one did in gaps between the real life of one's own studio time. He had a generous will to engage with the forming mind of the student, to challenge (and be challenged), to argue, theorize, reject, to get down on the studio floor and show by example.

Though the Borough Polytechnic was not a 'leading' institution like St Martin's or the Slade, its atmosphere had promise. London art schools were, as Auerbach points out, 'wide open after the War'. They held a mixture of ages and generations, part-time and full-time students, many of whom were foreigners – Auerbach remembers a large proportion of American ex-servicemen and refugee Polish girls at the Borough – so that the young students were always in contact with older ones 'who actually were serious about life, and had seen a lot of it . . . also, as was the case everywhere in postwar England, there was a very strong feeling that everyone had the *right* to an education.' The human material Bomberg had to work on, therefore, was by no means all bland or babyish. Nor was it infected with the narcissistic cult of creativity-as-therapy which, twenty years later, would help wreck the standards of late modernist art education in America. With Bomberg, learning was a battle; one needed resilience and bloody-mindedness to survive him.

His insecure domain was the engineering workshop of the Borough, which had been turned into its painting studio: a draughty space with echoing tiled walls, high ceilings and a sawtooth truss roof, whose door, like the bar doors in a Wild West saloon, kept clapping to and fro after one walked through it. There Bomberg held his life class. Auerbach had never heard of him before and his first impression was of 'a middle-aged man – he looked oldish to me, of course – in a white smock, grubby, bald and small'. He was

a person who certainly made no attempt to impress, except that when one began to talk to him one realized that he was quite exceptionally alive and full of energy. It took me some time to realize that he was the most formidably intelligent person I ever met in an art school.

Bomberg spoke to students as equals. He would say anything that came into his head and expect us to do the same. I felt then, as I feel now, that probably the way of address that had been present in London in the Vorticist days before World War I was preserved in him, in all its directness. Ezra Pound would tell someone like Yeats, straight to his face, that his poetry was rubbish; I believe he once scribbled the word *Putrid!* on Yeats's manuscript of 'The Tower' before sending it back to him. According to Wyndham Lewis, Gaudier-Breszka would hit Bomberg every time he saw him, simply because he didn't like his manner. There was a general feeling that it was possible, in fact absolutely mandatory, to say anything that you thought; that theories *as such* were immensely interesting and could be furiously debated, and that no one would take offence at the results.

Auerbach remembers no overriding orthodoxy in Bomberg's class. 'There are people now who claim that something is the case because "this is what David Bomberg advocated". But Bomberg himself never referred to anyone *else's* tenets as being the thing to conform to. Like every religious order, I suppose, like every innovative movement in art and ideas, what was actually an improvised, energetic, fresh leap into the unknown has been turned into an orthodoxy by followers. The classes were exceptionally free.' Bomberg's students tended to draw in charcoal on large sheets of paper, rather than in pencil or ink on small ones, but Auerbach does not remember any pressure to do so beyond the circumstance that 'working with large brushes or sticks of charcoal, in an improvisatory way, was partly forced by the fact that model sittings were very short and Bomberg only taught one day and two evenings a week. It wasn't a continuous course, and this encouraged one to work fast.'

One result of this leaning towards speed and emphatic gesture was a distant resemblance between the work of Bomberg's students and that of certain members of the New York School, of whom, in the late 40s, practically no one in England (and certainly no art students) had even heard. Auerbach remembers his fellow-student Gustave Metzger, proponent of 'auto-destructive art' in the 60s, painting 'in total innocence, three black eggs on a sheet of metal, rather like one of Motherwell's *Spanish Elegies*'. Other students struggled with five-inch-wide brushes on boards 'to pin down the most economical rhythm that defines the mass of the figure', and so produced images quite close to Franz Kline's. These resemblances were not due to some undercurrent of fashion, but neither were they accidental: Auerbach thinks they arose because 'people faced with a similar problem, whether they were in London or New York – that is, faced with an art that had become rather mannered, with a curious 'modernistic', late-Cubist vocabulary, as so much art in the late 30s and 40s had become – would hope to strike through to something more essential, less uniform, less armoured with chic, and try to get back to some kind of raw impulse. So the resemblances were adventitious by-products of what was, philosophically, a very serious longing to get back into a profound contact with the natural world.'

Auerbach started in the beginner's year at St Martin's School of Art in September 1948; he would study there for the next four years, and then at the Royal College of Art for another three, graduating from the latter in 1955 with a silver medal and first-class honours. For most of this irksomely long apprenticeship he would go to Bomberg's evening classes at the Borough Polytechnic as well. Before long he had persuaded Kossoff, then one year above him at St Martin's, to join them as well. Kossoff had served in the War; he was five years older than Auerbach, 'and so he had a much clearer sense of who he was than I did.' They both disliked the examination framework at St Martin's. 'I think Leon and I were perhaps a bit rougher and more rebellious than the other students. We wanted something a little less urbane, a little less tea-time, a little less limited. And not so linear and illustrative.' Kossoff's work of the time looked bigger and more daring then than it would today. One of the few works by another artist in Auerbach's studio is an early student Kossoff (1949) of a coal-delivery man with his horse-drawn cart, a small, brown image muffled in the vehemence of its own facture, about 30 × 22 inches. He remembers it looking 'quite exceptional, raw and large-scale' when he saw it at St Martin's, where the Intermediate test compositions were meant to be half that size, 22 × 15 inches. Kossoff failed the year. 'I had a very limited art education, but I knew what artists were! Artists were people who failed exams, got thrown out of art school, and were not subservient to their teachers – I recognized a certain magnanimity of talent in Kossoff.'

Kossoff and Auerbach would remain the closest of friends thereafter, through thick and thin – in terms of money, mostly thin. In time their differences of temperament would be clearly set forth in their work. Auerbach's overriding sense of being alone in the world would show in his attachment to the single, isolated figure, seen over and over again, re-imagined each time as unique and extraordinary. Auerbach's interest in narrative was slight. He would never try to paint people in social action. He tried to paint a crowd just once (in *Gaumont Cinema, Camden Town*, 1963). Even groups of figures are rare in his work – there are, in all, only seven such paintings: two versions of *E.O.W., S.A.W. and J.J.W. in the Garden*, 1963–64, two of *St Pancras Steps*, 1978–79, two of *Euston Steps*, 1981, and *Interior, Vincent Terrace II*, 1984. But the figures appear isolated. The single figure, theatrically lit, standing forth from its background, given weight and density by the material force of pigment, would be the basis of his art.

2 St Pancras Steps 1978–79

Kossoff, on the other hand, drew heavily on his collective experience as an East End Jew, the son of a baker whose cultural background – like Bomberg's own – was permeated with memories of the *stetl*, its closeness, its tribal interdependence. What the single figure became to Auerbach, the family unit was to Kossoff, whose paintings of his parents make up one of the few powerful meditations on age and need in twentieth-century art. His scenes of common London life, in public baths, markets and Underground entrances, are packed to distension with small figures, never disposed in a manner that suggests any kind of hierarchy or social grading. They seem mutually burdened, unable to escape either the closeness or the sufferings of their social matrix. They are stuck in Kossoff's dense paint like insects in jam. The atmosphere of Kossoff's social imagery faithfully reflects the democratic traditions of the *stetl*, in which, as Michael Roemer once pointed out, 'distinctions between people were far less important than common bonds and a shared destiny':

A Hassidic rabbi said: 'If the Messiah comes to you and says, "You are better than the others", you must say to him: "You're not the Messiah."' In Hebrew the word *olam* means not only 'world, universe' but also 'crowd, throng, people'. The world *is* people and the painter – like his subject – is one of the people: *ahad ha'am*.[16]

Between 1948 and 1953 Kossoff and Auerbach worked continuously together, roaming London in quest of motifs, drawing scenes from Hampstead Heath to the Smithfield meat markets. (With another art student, Philip Holmes, they formed 'a tiny gang'.) But their main bond was night class with Bomberg. Before long Auerbach realized that he was doing one kind of drawing at St Martin's and another at Bomberg's classes, 'and I felt the tug of both . . . At St Martin's I was learning to make a compromise with what I felt, in order to make something logical and coherent and understood. With Bomberg I was making no compromise at all with my reactions, but

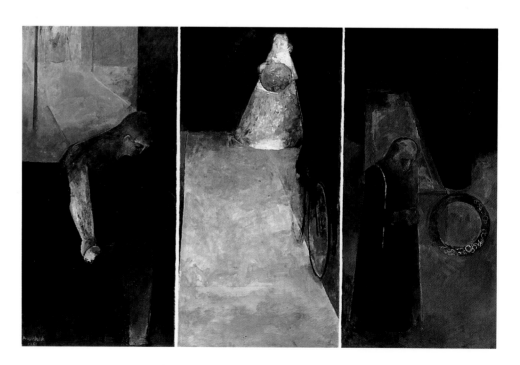

3 Birth, Marriage, Death 1951

rejecting the chance of getting something complex and explicit.' The influence of his St Martin's training can be seen in a very formal triptych of birth, marriage and death, squared up from preliminary drawings in 1951, thinly painted, and full of coltish, earnest museum references: Rembrandt's *Jewish Bride*, for instance, is the source of the betrothed couple in the 'marriage' panel, for which Auerbach posed in a mirror with a girlfriend.

The results of Bomberg's teaching were altogether different. A hard critic, Bomberg would not let his students fudge. He prodded them to 'define their experience of matter'. He wanted them, Auerbach recalls, 'actually to apprehend the weight, the twist, the stance, of a human being anchored by gravity: to produce a souvenir of that'.

He tried to get them to think of form in terms of vectors, thrusts and densities rather than the membrane of flattened boxes that was the typical space of Cubist-influenced painting in England. He kept driving home the point that 'the eye is a stupid organ', whose impressions needed to be reinforced by the other senses, especially that of touch: what depictive art needed was an existential solidity, groped out part by part, as a person feels his way around a dark room:

He spoke of drawing as being simply a question of getting a set of directions for the full 360° around the object. And he didn't believe in modelling the thing up artificially to give it weight. Weight was something you *felt* – it couldn't be feigned. Nor did he believe in making curlicues to produce a beautifully shaped leg. He decried that as facility. It was the sort of thing Augustus John would do. He was most disparaging about John. He called him the poor man's Ingres. . . .

In some ways Bomberg's effect on his students at the Polytechnic, and on Kossoff and Auerbach in particular, resembled the impact F. R. Leavis (1895–1978) had on successive generations of Eng. Lit. students at Cambridge, with the difference that Leavis had many more followers in his own lifetime. Each man believed himself to be insufficiently recognized outside his own small *cénacle* (only Bomberg was right in this) and both evoked extremes of devotion and antagonism. Neither made a secret of his antipathies: both thought Bloomsbury had poisoned English culture with élitism and dilettantism. Bomberg had no modern painter he felt he could point to as a supreme example of aesthetic probity, as Leavis had D. H. Lawrence – 'Actually', says Auerbach, 'Bomberg felt he was his own Lawrence.' But there was in both men a sense of near-Messianic urgency, of the Word being passed from master to apprentice; a passion for the 'organic' and 'direct' as against the mannered or abstracted. And there was the same awkwardness and stubbornness in the sight of an original mind laboriously making the tools for itself before fashioning the object of thought. 'You could tell a piece of Leavis almost anywhere', Auerbach says, 'with its peculiar grinding cack-handedness and heaviness of syntax, partly because he was chewing out his own definitions. Bomberg's conversation, too, would be fairly impenetrable to outsiders unless they had patience with him or, as in my case, were young enough to have become habituated to it. He spoke on his own terms, and didn't take anything over from other people without examining and remaking it.' One example of his penchant for the gnomic and overcompressed was a definition of painting as 'A tone of day or night and the monument to a memorable hour. It is structure in textures of colour.'[17]

Bomberg had no philosophical pretensions – 'he was immensely fluent, but only intermittently logically articulate' – but he held strong views on the nature of perception and these suffused both his painting and his teaching. In large part they derived from Bishop Berkeley:

> The point about Berkeley's philosophy of seeing, as Bomberg grasped it, was that human beings only learn to connect sight to their experience of the physical world by a fairly long experimentation with touch and the other senses. The retina reverses things, like a concave lens. On the back of the retina we get a reverse image, so that the newborn infant will reach down for something that's up and up for something that's down. It's only by crawling across the floor, touching things, judging distances *haptically*, by grasp and contact, that it will relate the sight to the physical world.

Thus touch, for Auerbach's understanding of Bomberg, was the primary regulator of sight. 'We elucidate the sight from the memory of touch, and out of our understanding of that architecture we then make an image out of lines and other marks. The rest will come to you; you find yourself making gestures that imply legs and breasts and so on, you find yourself creating a sense of mass on the flat surface simply because you felt it. Bomberg's idea of "the spirit in the mass" was bound up with that: the very particular, very exact expression of the object you're painting. You're most likely to get it right when you're least self-conscious, when you have given up any hope of producing an acceptable image – because then you're permeated wordlessly by the influence of the thing you're painting.'

Bomberg's teaching method, then, had less to do with showing people how to produce aesthetically efficient pictures than with trying to instil 'a sense of the quality of form'. He never talked about subject-matter – a question which Auerbach regards as central to painting – and 'he didn't talk about certain things which I think he took for granted, such as the momentousness for the artist of his subject', because

> it was so deeply in him that he never felt the need to articulate it. What happened was that people would draw. As soon as they seemed to be drawing in a way that was bitty, affected, mannered or using a cliché learned from art, he would refer them back to the model and . . . suggest a total destruction, and they would destroy it and go on; and probably where they were not in the least aware of having done a picture he might stop suddenly and say, 'There is some quality in this form.' [The resulting work] had very little sense of responsible achievement by the artist, but it bore within it a hint, no more, of something very grand, noble and profound in painting, so that, from my personal point of view, they would not be *paintings* or *images* but they would carry in them hints of a language of greater depth, freedom and courage than most of the achieved art then being created in other places in England.[18]

Here lay some of the roots of the slow, opaque tactility of Auerbach's early work in the 50s; its mortared, wall-like surface; its rebarbative earnestness. But Auerbach was far more influenced by Bomberg the teacher than by Bomberg the painter – by his precepts rather than his practice. He points out that 'the deep necessity I have to get profoundly involved with the subject is something I certainly didn't learn from Bomberg.' Bomberg painted fast, and though he passed months at a time so distracted that he could not touch a brush, he had produced thousands of drawings and perhaps a thousand paintings by the end of his life. Auerbach was slow, not by choice but by temperament; he could not help it. 'It was only after I left art school that I realized it was all right not to finish a painting in a night, or a week, or in the four weeks a model would pose. Very often it took me years to do. I didn't do a drawing in a day, which was the optimum time. It took me many sittings to do a drawing I valued.'

Mainly, Bomberg taught Auerbach and Kossoff to go against the grain. Failure seemed 'natural' to them: 'Leon and I, when we were students, simply assumed persistence, obscurity, the making of *le chef-d'oeuvre inconnu*. But with persistence things do change.' The point was to keep going, and the problem of how to do that produced a severe crisis for Auerbach when, in 1952, he finished at St Martin's and prepared to move to the Royal College of Art. He was now twenty-one and, the law said, he must do National Service for two years in the British Army. 'I'd been in institutions for five years, which seemed a century to me. I felt I would be doomed if I went into the Army. I also felt I'd be doomed if I went to the Royal College and just became an art student for another three years.' Auerbach set out to fail his medical examination and failed so well that he was classified D4, totally unfit for active military service. In the summer, before classes at the Royal College began, he did odd jobs to survive. He ran a bagatelle stall at the Battersea fun-fair on Fridays and Saturdays, drew catalogue bicycles on a duplicator for a Nigerian businessman, and worried about the future:

I needed the tension, the research and study, that the semi-academic education at St Martin's had implied. It was never very thorough in an academic sense – but it was a whole sight more academically thorough than any art education that's offered today. We did anatomy, for instance. We did a lot of drawing, from models, in the zoo, and so on. Education guarantees nothing; it just gives a chance to those who want to learn to later learn something. It didn't do more than that. I needed that sort of attention to the specific.

But of course I absolutely needed the feeling of breaking through into uncharted territory, and working in a world where no rules were known and anything was possible. I had caught a glimpse of that in Bomberg's classes: a larger improvisation of gestures that might pull forms out of thin air.

Auerbach sensed it would not be easy to keep these together now across three more years of study. The Royal College of Art term began on 1 September 1952. On the first day Auerbach went with other new students to the school commissary and was primly issued with six small tubes of oil-colour. 'Even then, it seemed so ridiculously inadequate. I felt disgusted entering an institution again, becoming a student once more, thinking I would have to conform in some way and compromise again.' Fuming inside, he stalked home to Walham Green and found that, in his temper, he was able to finish a small painting he had been stalled on for weeks, and whose completion seemed to mark (however unassumingly) the beginning of his life as an artist. The subject was a building site in the Earl's Court Road. Auerbach had been there many times to make notes of its elements: the deep diagonal cut of the excavations, the small labouring figures and especially – by the instinctive stroke that lays open a peep, no more, at work to come – the triangular ladders and emphatic horizontal–vertical scaffolding that would predict the pictorial construction of his later paintings. He wanted prismatic colour, a space defined entirely by colour: 'Making space with colour was very much in the air then, and I took it in as an idea before I could really articulate it – at least it was more interesting than making an illustrative grid and covering that with some sort of colour. I was very interested in [the colour of] Ivon Hitchens.' Today the grid of *Summer Building Site*, 1952, does look fairly illustrative, but its chrome yellow diagonals and the little red figures of bricklayer and hodman looked promisingly raw at the time and already, in the impasto with which the vertical columns and the legs of ladders that lock the centre of the painting together are rendered, there is a premonition (no more than that) of the thick surfaces to come. 'Not until the very end did I get the courage to make some things bigger and others smaller than they were, to get the expression of the whole thing . . . When I had done it I recognized somehow that I had cut through my habits, I had made some shapes that seemed to conjure up a coherent plastic fact: I had done my own painting. I didn't know whether I would ever be able to do it again, but at least I knew what it felt like.'[19]

Colour Plates

1952 ~ 70

4 Summer Building Site 1952

5 E.O.W. Nude 1953–54

6 Head of Leon Kossoff 1954

7 Head of E.O.W. 1955

8 Head of E.O.W. 1954

9 Head of E.O.W. 1957

10 E.O.W., Half-length Nude 1958

11 Oxford Street Building Site II 1959–61

12 Head of E.O.W. II 1961

13 Study after Deposition by Rembrandt II 1961

14 Nude on Bed II 1961

15 Head of E.O.W. VI 1961

16 Head of E.O.W. V 1961

17 Smithfield Meat Market 1962

18 View from Primrose Hill 1963

19 Head of Gerda Boehm II 1963

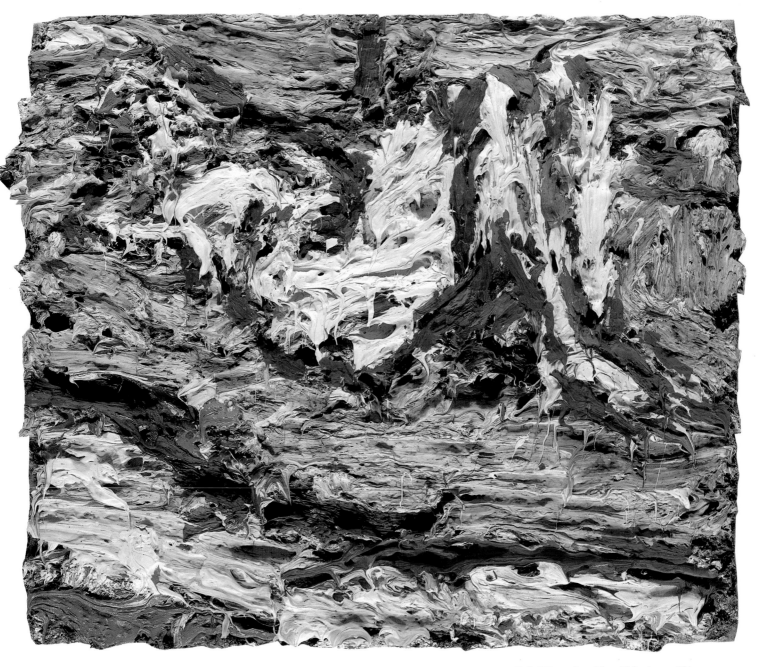

20 E.O.W. on her Blue Eiderdown VI 1963

21 Gaumont Cinema, Camden Town 1963

22 The Sitting Room 1964

23 E.O.W., S.A.W. and J.J.W. in the Garden I 1963

24 E.O.W., S.A.W. and J.J.W. in the Garden II 1964

25 Head of E.O.W. III 1963–64

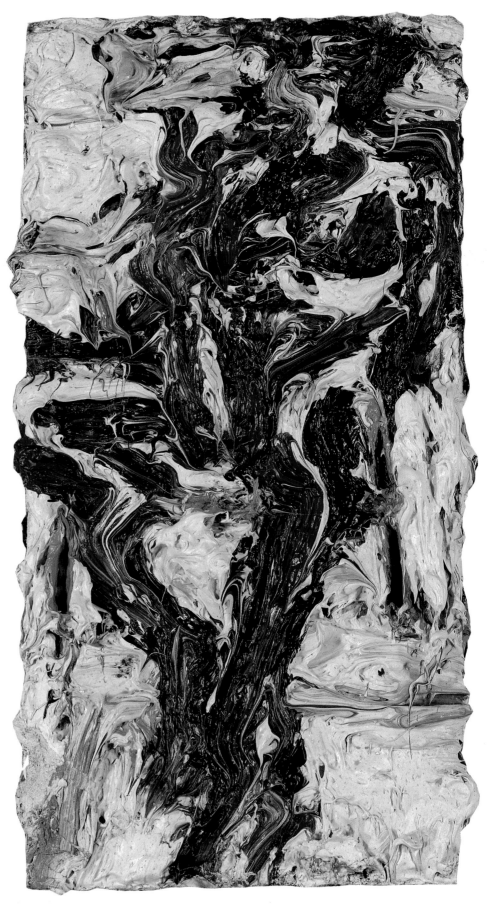

26 Seated Model in Studio IV 1964

27 Portrait of Helen Gillespie I 1964

28 Study after Titian II, Tarquin and Lucrece 1965

29 E.O.W. on her Blue Eiderdown II 1965

30 E.O.W. on her Blue Eiderdown 1965

31 E.O.W., Head on her Pillow III 1966

32 Studio with Figure on Bed II 1966

33 Reclining Figure in the Studio 1966

34 E.O.W. Sleeping 1966

35 Mornington Crescent IV 1967

36 Mornington Crescent 1967

37 Head of Miss Steinberg 1967

38 Figure on a Bed 1968

39 Primrose Hill 1968

40 Primrose Hill, Autumn Morning 1968

41 The Origin of the Great Bear 1968

42 Mornington Crescent – Winter 1969

43 E.O.W. Reclining 1970

VII

The Royal College of Art turned out to be a strikingly liberal school. Intelligent teachers like John Minton and Rodrigo Moynihan took some interest in its students, but put no pressure on them. Auerbach found that he could paint at home in his rented room, and use the college only for drawing from the model. In this way, between 1952 and 1955, Auerbach began to make his own sense out of the influence of Bomberg and others.

The earliest Auerbachs, like *Seated Man*, 1950, are Bombergian in their vehement scaffolding of dark shadow, thrusting the light planes of shoulder and shin forward. Such drawings as *Portrait of Leon Kossoff*, 1951, and *Woman with Hands Clasped on Head*, 1951, reflect Bomberg's emphasis on the quick grasp of 'essential' planes, the lights cut from the charcoal with an eraser. By now Auerbach was using almost geometrical shapes, like the triangles of the nude's raised arms that repeat, and balance, the heavy triangular plane of her thigh — a pear-shaped mass whose rootedness is increased by the downward pull of the white strokes. A sense of scaffolding is in the surface. The paintings were more turgid, less linear. In *E.O.W. Nude*, 1952, the figure barely emerges from honey-coloured mud. A *Head of E.O.W.* from the next year is flatter and a Bombergian wedge of light descends from the nose and cuts irrationally across the jawline. But from here on the paint thickens, the form of the head becomes static, like that of some archaic effigy dredged from the seabed, half-effaced by calcinations — the pigment.

'I was born old, and I wanted to make a dignified perverse image, a formal image.' By 1954–55 he knew he had to do it by painting something specific and unvarying — over and over and over again. Reiteration went against the ideal of virtuosity shared by many young English artists after the war:

> . . . in the early 50s there was talk of people painting a show in three months, or something like that, which seemed to me somehow to be superficial and illustrative and deedy and skimpy and just simply not what paintings require . . . part of this instinct of revulsion against the current art may have produced in me a strong feeling that one would try to emphasize what was more permanent than a decorative or linear concoction. This was massive substance . . . this was the permanence. This was where the energy came from, and it may be the thickness of the paint was something to do with this since my way of painting is not a question of choosing a uniform . . . I can now see why people thought there was something blatant and indigestible about [my early paintings]. But I can assure you that when I did them they simply felt to me to be true.[20]

He was lucky to find support and reassurance for this odd ambition from a dealer, Helen Lessore, who ran the Beaux-Arts Gallery in London and gave him his first solo show in January 1956. The idealism of this older woman reminded him of Anna Essinger:

44 Seated Man 1950

45 Woman with Hands Clasped on Head 1951

46 E.O.W. Nude 1952

47 Portrait of Leon Kossoff 1951

48 Head of E.O.W. 1953

There wasn't the slightest disjunction between what [Lessore] believed, what she said, and what she did. It was not unlike Bunce Court! — including the fact that I felt perfectly at home there, she was like Tanta Anna: she was quite sure that what she wanted had an absolute moral sanction. In that sense I felt quite at home.

One photo of Lessore seems to sum up the character she reluctantly displayed to the art world of the 50s. It is taken in the upper room of the Beaux-Arts Gallery, and she is sitting in front of her desk on the edge of the day-bed. She is soberly dressed. She fixes the camera with a pale, resigned stare, as though being photographed were like a visit to the dentist. Her hands are clasped in her lap. Her feet, hearsed in blunt shiny shoes, are close together. (Andrew Forge wrote that, when you went downstairs at the Beaux-Arts Gallery, 'Mrs Lessore's shoes would watch you go.') She is the art-nun personified. Anything less like today's image of the woman art-dealer would be hard to imagine.

But then, Lessore disliked the commerce of the art world. To be with her, an artist needed a stoic indifference to the pangs of ambition. Soon after closing the Beaux-Arts Gallery in 1965 — a time when selling contemporary art was still a soft business, compared to today — she was asked to lecture at an art school on her experiences as a dealer. She refused with a note:

Reading the letters of van Gogh or the novels of Zola one might not think that the behaviour of art dealers, and of official bodies, has changed much; and yet it has . . . the whole art world has become like a *maison de haute couture* — it has become more grossly commercial than it used to be even thirty years ago — even fifteen years ago — more superficial, more vulgar, more greedy . . .

I cannot stand up and tell the students what they must do to be 'successful'; nor have I the heart . . . to stand there and exhort these hopeful young things to take the martyr's road.[21]

Born Helen Brook, Lessore started as a painter but married into art dealing: her husband Major Frederick Lessore, himself a sculptor, owned the Beaux-Arts Gallery and she kept it running after he died in 1951. In business she was both scrupulous and rather amateurish. She meant a great deal to 'her' artists (among whom, between 1952 and 1965, were her son John Lessore, Kossoff, Craigie Aitchison, Raymond Mason, John Bratby, Michael Andrews and Francis Bacon), and certainly to Auerbach:

She was, after all, a painter. There was no uncertainty in her mind as to what she liked. The most important thing was that if a painter was doing badly in the world, she would if anything support him more. If there was no critical response, if nothing sold, her support would be doubled rather than lessened. It was an extraordinary human quality. She liked what she believed in and she liked it better if nobody else liked it. If people were doing well she would sometimes cool slightly towards them; she felt a little as though something were being taken away from her. At the end, when she was distracted by money worries and other problems and she knew she was going to close the gallery, she sent me a cheque for a hundred pounds for nothing —

even though I hoped to join another gallery; when Marlborough took me on I returned the cheque.

In 1955 Lessore visited the final examination exhibition at the Royal College of Art. She wrote to four of its exhibitors (Keith Cunningham, Michael Pope, Joe Tilson and Auerbach) and offered to put their work into her next summer show. Then she went round to Auerbach's studio and bought six of his paintings for sixty pounds. She continued to show his work until the gallery closed.

If the Beaux-Arts Gallery's artists formed a group, it was not at all coherent. Mainly they had in common the fact that Lessore, most of the time, liked heightened forms of figuration with a base in past art. 'She showed all sorts of people, some of them in my view not very remarkable', according to Auerbach:

I am sure Helen wanted to make the gallery stand for *something*, though. There was no question of it being a job, it was her life. Perhaps there was a touch of Bloomsbury-as-it-used-to-be. She would give me one large mug of French coffee with chicory, and look at what I'd brought in; it was very touching, unlike any other gallery — more extreme, perhaps; if she was pleased and moved by the painting I'd brought in, it was almost as if one had made a woman happy in some other way. It would make her day. Her connection with the gallery came from deep feelings. You felt she might go on you or she might go off you — it could make a lot of difference; and there was, there couldn't help but be, a slight undercurrent of rivalry between her artists for that reason. Some saw one another regularly, others not at all. But it wasn't a group.

Years later, Lessore wrote about visiting Auerbach's studio for the first time in the summer of 1955, and the 'extraordinary effect' of his early landscapes of Primrose Hill, 'all in yellow ochre, grooved, engraved, as if in wet gravelly sand: as if one had fallen asleep after long contemplation of some Rembrandt with a glimpse of mysterious parkland in the golden-brown distance, and then in a dream found oneself actually walking in the landscape.' She saw what would elude most others for the next fifteen years: that the goal of Auerbach's talent was stillness and definition, something inward and 'natural' rather than rhetorical and 'expressionist'.

The palette of these early works is black and white, and earth colours ranging from yellow ochre to a dark greenish umber. These were the only pigments Auerbach could afford to buy in quantity. But if the range of colour was curtailed, that of surface was not. Auerbach's 1954 portraits of Kossoff — especially the large head painted on board, an image several times life-size — are relentless but frustrated in their scrutiny. The head fills the frame, edge to edge, and seems all the more massive for the paint's denseness; yet its solidity is contradicted by the shifting textures, clots and waxy lumps of pigment, and by the way in which Auerbach plays down the expression of his sitter's face (the nose a wedge, the mouth a slit) but plays up the strange silvery light that radiates from the visual node of the painting, Kossoff's forehead. It says nothing about the character, the feelings or even the sexual identity of the sitter. Its point lies in archaic stoniness, and ineloquence.

So with other portraits: though *Head of E.O.W.*, 1954, has its tenderness – with the inclination of the head, the accidental similarity of the turban of hair to a dark aureole, and the faint flush of rose in the cheek, it distantly suggests the head of a *trecento* Madonna and reminds one of how impressed Auerbach had been by the formal grandeur of Giotto – the 1955 *Head of E.O.W.* is so severe that one can hardly recognize this face, at first, as being a woman's.

As in the large portrait of Kossoff (but with more refinement) the weight of the image is in the upper part of the head, the massive cranium and brow, whose proportions are so increased as to exceed, in depth, the 'expressive' half of the face below the eyebrows. This was an echo of Rembrandt's *Jakob Trip*, which he had studied in the National Gallery – the gleam of light from the great domed forehead, setting both the scale of luminosity of the image and its content, the praise of inward reflection. On the one hand, the head is vehement, both as surface (each blob and strand of pigment is thrust towards the eye as if by fermentation below) and as structure: the big grooved plane of the forehead, the encircling coil of hair, the jut of the orbital ridges and the shadow under the cheekbone. On the other, it is curiously elusive. E.O.W.'s gaze does not meet one's own; the eyes are cavities, the mouth another slit, the expression unreadable. Reality for Auerbach, even at this stage, is dense, violently alive but remote – something to be dug out through many layers.

The sign of this excavation, the sludge from which body or landscape were made, was the glistening, granular surface, an inch thick. Paint would always be the first thing one saw in an early Auerbach. Certainly it was for me, five years later: the first Auerbach I saw was *Oxford Street Building Site II*, 1959–61, bought by the National Gallery of Victoria in Australia. When it went up on the wall in the Australian summer it was still not dry; one poked it with an inquisitive finger and the paint surface gave, like human skin. Nobody who saw it then had ever imagined that such a thick

49 Head of Leon Kossoff 1954

surface could be made out of oil-paint. At night, rumour said, the Auerbach crept: a wave of sticky pigment crawled downwards, lapping over the frame. It was whispered that the Melbourne museum, despairing of any cure and unable to make the paint dry any faster, stored the thing upside down (as befitted the Antipodes) in the hope that gravity would pull it back into shape. None of this art-student folklore turned out to be true. *Oxford Street Building Site II* is still in Melbourne, right way up, dry after twenty-six years, and in fine shape.

Now thick-surface painting was very much in the air on both sides of the Channel in the late 50s and early 60s. The English audience knew Fautrier's amorphous slabs of gesso tinted with thin washes and scrubbings of pigment, and Dubuffet's portraits, cows and *texturologies*, their designs scribed into the thick surface of sand and paint.

But when Auerbach had has first show at the Beaux-Arts Gallery in January 1956, all the London critics except one were nonplussed by the paint. 'The thickest pictures that anyone is ever likely to see', wrote John Russell. 'The eye flounders.' The *Manchester Guardian* found his technique 'fantastically obtrusive'. *The Times* thought it 'laborious, clumsy and not very eloquent'.[22] Real support came from David Sylvester, who went out on a limb and hailed the show in *The Listener* as 'the most exciting and impressive first one-man show by an English painter since Francis Bacon in 1949', detecting in it an awkward sentimentality but also 'the qualities that make for greatness in a painter – fearlessness; a profound originality; a total absorption in what obsesses him; and, above all, a certain authority and gravity in his forms and colours.' In particular Sylvester was careful to distinguish the peculiar qualities of Auerbach's thick paint from the thickness of other *bas-relief* surfaces, having in mind the work of Dubuffet, which had just been seen in depth for the first time in England at the I.C.A. the year before:

> . . . in spite of the heaped-up paint, these are painterly images, not sculptural ones, have to be read as paintings, not as polychrome reliefs, and make their point just because their physical structure is virtually that of sculpture but their psychological impact is that of painting . . . in this clotted heap of muck there has somehow been preserved the precious fluidity, the pliancy proper to paint.[23]

Sylvester had grasped that Auerbach's surfaces retained the essential character of paint as a substance which stores and emits light. With Tàpies or Dubuffet, this was not so. Their 'matter painting' was basically relief sculpture, with incisions, drawing and tints. Plopped or trowelled onto the surface like stucco, it seemed to have been broken off the real world – a sample, not an illusion, of reality. However, in claiming to be part of the stuff of the world, like the cracked plaster on a Catalan wall (Tàpies) or a dried cowpat (Dubuffet) it gave up other kinds of illusion. The thickness and rigidity of the crust were symbolic ends in themselves. You could not look *through* them, which was the point of Auerbach's surface – its peculiar alternation between opaque mud and a contained light, locked glimmering within it. Kossoff would later describe the effect:

> . . . in spite of the excessive piling on of paint, the effect of these works on the mind is of images recovered and reconceived in the barest and most particular light, the same

light that seems to glow through the late, great, thin Turners. This light, which gleams through the thickness and finally remains with us is an unpremeditated manifestation arising from the constant application of true draughtsmanship.[24]

The paint's assertiveness was misread as a mimicry of bas-relief sculpture and even as a sign of manual virtue, as though Auerbach put it there to prove he 'tried hard'. Freudians pounced on it as symbolic shit – all that brown stuff, squeezed from tubes onto the same spot, day after day! They had a point, since the infant's desire to hoard and show his faeces (his first product) is connected to the desire for security which ran through Auerbach's orphanhood and moulded his habits as an artist. But this line of enquiry does not take one very far since, as Andrew Forge observed in 1963, it says little about the particular properties of Auerbach's work: 'a willingness to see oil paint as ideal faeces is probably as old as the medium and is just as likely to be at work in the amateur painting weekend in the vicarage garden as it is here. The only thing that is special about Auerbach in this connection is his extremism, and to understand this we have to look elsewhere.'[25]

In the midst of their differences Kossoff and Auerbach had one subject in common – London itself. Their city was a commoner place than the ordered array of Georgian housefronts and squares beloved of tourist and topographer – a city of work, not cultural spectacle, mournful in weather and silvery of light, gapped like a boxer's mouth by German bombs and not yet repaired. Kossoff movingly recalled his feelings about this city:

> I was born in a now demolished building in City Road not far from St Paul's. Ever since the age of twelve I have drawn and painted London. I have worked from Bethnal Green, the City, Willesden Junction, York Way, and Dalston. I have painted its bombed sites, building sites, excavations, railways and recently a children's swimming-pool in Willesden.
>
> The strange, ever changing light, the endless streets and the shuddering feel of the sprawling city linger in my mind like a faintly glimmering memory of a long forgotten, perhaps never experienced childhood which, if rediscovered and illuminated, would ameliorate the pain of the present.[26]

Auerbach's attachment to London was just as strong. The emigrant's anxiety kept him there, with his nose to the streets and parks; he was not only a 'born-again Englishman', as he once put it, but a born-again Londoner, who acquired all his cultural baggage in the city and would not leave it. 'I hate leaving my studio, I hate leaving [Camden Town], I hate leaving London. I don't think I've spent more than four weeks abroad since I was seven.'[27]

The modern form of some cities has been recorded by painters. The archetype is Paris, whose changes after 1850 were painted in detail – parks, boulevards, bridges, railway stations, excavations, monuments, café life and all – by *boulevardier* artists and Impressionists. Some images by Joseph Stella, Stuart Davis and Georgia O'Keeffe are vivid reminders of New York's lyric prometheanism in the 20s and 30s. The bewildering sprawl of Los Angeles is given sharp iconic form by David Hockney's palms and blue swimming-pools. But amorphous London, the great grey palimpsest, is not a city of that kind – or so it seemed, and still seems, to Auerbach:

> I have a strong sense that London hasn't been properly painted. New York has been – think of Stella's *Brooklyn Bridge*, or O'Keeffe's *Shelton with Sunspots*. Paris has been painted to the last detail. But London? Monet on the Thames, Derain at the docks; bits and pieces, rather spottily, by Whistler and Sickert. But it has always cried out to be painted, and not been. The things Rimbaud and Verlaine felt about it! They cried out to be recorded and preserved against time!

And yet Auerbach had little of the topographer in him. He did not move around much, or care about variety. In later years he would paint three motifs, over and over. One was, and is, the park at Primrose Hill. The second was the corner of Camden High Street and Mornington Crescent. The third was the entrance to his own studio.

But in the 50s he mainly painted holes in the ground. Sites in the centre of London, bombed flat, were then being dug out and rebuilt. The excavations, chasms of mud and shored-up earth, overhung by cranes and crossed by scaffolding and catwalks, fascinated him – a triangulated structure, a diagram that reminded him of the vectoring forms he had learned about from Bomberg and which were becoming the stylistic signature of his work, laid over the primal clay of the city. This was a scene unlike the Arcadian landscapes favoured by older English painters – John Piper's cathedrals and towers, John Craxton's Greek hillsides with Picassian goats – but it was intensely picturesque (new ruins, still reeking of catastrophe) and its sense of incoherence slowly labouring to give birth to structural shape matched the processes in which, Auerbach had by now realized, his own work was grounded.

50 St Pancras Building Site, Summer 1954

So he was drawn to the craters of Oxford Street and the new Shell building rising on the devastated bank of the Thames. They were scenery, a link between his interest in theatre and Piranesi's *Carceri d'Invenzione*, which Bomberg, he says, had shown him 'quite early on': 'I would go and draw them by inching along the planks, out over the excavation, just clinging on and dodging the wheelbarrows. I have no head for heights. Everything you can be frightened of, I am — I can't even swim.'

The results were clumsy at first; none of the spatial vertigo Auerbach mentions (a feeling which depends, above all, on the air's transparency) could find its way through the stolid surface of *St Pancras Building Site, Summer*, 1954, although more of it is apparent in the plunging orthogonals, the depth framed by the kite-shaped central form of *Shell Building Site from the Thames*, 1959. The heaviness of the surface is a charm *against* the fear of heights — it brings the eye, and with it one's tactile sense, right down to earth. One sees this plainly in *St Paul's Building Site, c.* 1955, in which there is almost no light at all, just a mass of black and dark umber pigment, a black criss-cross of lines ploughed through the leathery darkness, relieved only by a small flare of Indian red and a patch of nearly submerged French ultramarine. But by the end of the 50s, in such paintings as *Maples Demolition*, 1960, and especially the large *Oxford Street Building Sites* of 1959–61, his building-site images had developed a dogged eloquence. Now one is made to feel the damp on the tarpaulins and the slimy dunching of the deep London subsoil, see the tea-coloured light reflected from standing puddles, notice the specific forms of barrow, hod and girder. The space is flattened by the thickness of substance. There is no sky. The clay is reconstructed out of earth-colour, watery mud evoked by oily mud — ochre, umber, terre verte, Indian red. But whereas in earlier Auerbachs one was aware mainly of the thickness of the surface, one now sees the directions and vectors of the drawings working fully in the thickness of paint. Wide continuous tracks of the brush leave clearly defined raised edges in the paint around them, so that details seem inlaid, as in the

52 St Paul's Building Site *c.* 1955

53 Maples Demolition 1960

51 Oxford Street Building Site I 1959–60

beautifully rendered arabesque of cable in the lower left foregroud of *Oxford Street Building Site II*. The linear scaffolding of such pictures, heaving itself out of their dense paste, predicts a line of development in Auerbach's art, towards drawn forms that are both free and not free – the hooking brushstrokes that convey such muscular energy just because they are clotted, substantial and embedded in surface, not floating in air as 'calligraphy'. Auerbach still says he was surprised when people focussed on the thickness of his surface:

> I don't know how they can talk about thickness, really. Is blue better than red, thick better than thin? – no. But the sense of corporeal reality, that's what matters. English twentieth-century painting tends to be thin, linear and illustrative. I wanted something different; I wanted to make a painting that, when you saw it, would be like touching something in the dark. But Matisse could do that with thin paint and bright colours!

Like any young painter in the years of extreme curiosity – the twenties, when the mind takes impressions like wax and retains them like marble – Auerbach in the 50s looked at a great deal of art, took notes on it, made drawings from it, wrote poems about it, and gathered as many reproductions as he could afford. Then, as now, he had the habit of pulling out photos and plates apparently at random and dealing them across the floor when working 'to have something good to look at', although the image has nothing apparent to do with the painting in hand: a black-and-white photo of a Fang mask or of Vermeer's young turbaned girl, Michelangelo's Palestrina *Pietà*, a portrait by Titian. Sometimes one will substitute for another: once, plopping down by the easel's foot a catalogue open at Reynolds's self-portrait with a bust of Michelangelo, he remarked that 'I wanted to look at a Rembrandt but I couldn't find the one I wanted, so Reynolds has to do: it comes from Rembrandt's *Aristotle contemplating the Bust of Homer*, anyway.' Other habits have stuck: in the 50s, as still today, he would in any given week draw exhaustively from one painting in the National Gallery, no matter how unlike his own work it was – usually the further away the better, because the contrast stretched him. He made drawings, for instance, from Uccello's *Rout of San Romano* and Signorelli's *Circumcision*, paintings which bore no similarity to his own procedures.

Under such miscellaneous promptings, deeper affinities run. Auerbach has always denied, and with reason, that he is an 'expressionist' artist, but one of the painters he most loved in the 50s was Chaim Soutine – though not for the 'conventional' signs of expressive emotion recorded in Soutine's twisting brushmarks:

> I can't deny that Soutine had a very great effect on me, especially the Céret pictures. I can't think of him as an expressionist artist, but as a great draughtsman who follows the form around the back and out the other side. He was a better draughtsman than either Braque or Gris, neither of whom drew very well. There is absolutely *nothing* pedantic about Soutine's drawing; on the other hand, he didn't just make up shapes for the pleasure of making them up. One always feels a correspondence with the motif, at every point.

There were other reasons to identify with Soutine too: one exiled Jew, without money or influence, recognized the impulses of another. 'Soutine did poor artist's painting. Poor artist's painting has to do with material painted under great harrassment, as though if it weren't done *now* it would never be done. And though I can't claim to do so, it is not sentimental to say that there are artists who speak for the outcasts — even though so much *misérabliste* painting is sentimental, like most blue-period Picasso, or worse.'

Both he and Kossoff thought of Rembrandt a lot in the 50s — and ever since; they went to the National Gallery so often to study and draw from the *Portrait of Hendrickje Stoffels*, the *Bearded Man in a Cap*, the *Deposition*, the *Saskia as Flora*, the *Woman Bathing in a Stream*, both the self-portraits and both pictures of Margaretha de Geer that other friends of Kossoff would hear him say that 'Frank and I are the only people in England who *really* understand Rembrandt.' Auerbach did not think so, but Rembrandt set unnegotiable standards for him on several levels. There was the sense of iconic vitality that the quarter-length seated figure, staring frontally from dark space, could still contain. There was the glimmer of internal light bedded in the paint; and the jostle and tension of blunt marks within any given shape, a red corner of Turkey carpet in half-darkness or the fluting of a white ruff, that evinced layers of small structure resolved as directional paint-strokes. And there was the direct, seemingly unmediated way in which a square brushmark, not licked, could become the code of form, turning things parallel to the surface, making the back and fingers of a hand from shallow oblongs — structure and scaffolding all the way, even at the height of impasto. Above all, the man's control evoked Auerbach's wonder: 'The handling is so rapid and responsive, but the mind is that of a conceptualizing architect, making coherent geometries in space.' Over time, these matters would wind their way into Auerbach's own work.

He also thought a great deal about a neglected English artist: Walter Sickert. The Beaux-Arts Gallery had a talisman, which hung in Helen Lessore's bedroom. It was Sickert's self-portrait, *The Servant of Abraham*, 1929: the over-life-size head of the artist in his late sixties, bearded and patriarchal, slanting across the canvas as though Sickert had just spun on his heel to face an interruption, urgent and scrubby in facture — one of the masterpieces of his improvisatory late manner. Today Auerbach believes that 'the one painter of *real* world stature who worked in England in the early part of this century was Sickert', but until Lessore (whose husband had been Sickert's dealer) took Auerbach up he had not thought much about him, probably less than his fellow art students:

When I was a student many of the students around me were doing paintings of nudes on iron bedsteads, and I thought of that as a cosy, domestic let-out. My vision of painting, the picture I had in my head, was of some clearly formal statement; an explosion; and I thought there was something too domestic and whimsical and Impressionistic about Sickert. I remember reacting with considerable scepticism when Helen said he was the best.

The curious thing about people's taste in art is that the opinions one holds, and one's real attachments, are not necessarily the same thing — and the real attachments become apparent because one finds oneself returning to things that have no place in one's theoretical scheme of how art should be; one just finds oneself *not bored* with them, and coming back to them . . . Sickert's late pictures, especially, were very tough and there was nothing else in the least like them. He was marvellously formally inventive.

Sickert's critical essays, collected in 1947 under the title *A Free House* and long out of print, languished as unread as Ruskin's. Auerbach gobbled them up:

> I read his writings when I was a student. They worried me; I didn't think it proper to be reading them . . . perhaps one should be reading Apollinaire instead? But his energy and wit, and the optimism, and the considerable profundity in odd places just got through to me. I loved the book and I still do. When I find myself very tired of an afternoon I sometimes pick that book up and go to a page and read it, and I find it works for me – I just want to go on working. It's a matter of the man's all-round worth.

Between 1890 and 1914, through his friendship with Degas, Sickert became the main professional link between painting in Paris and London. He adopted Degas's pictorial construction, with its allusions to the snapshot, its empirical framing. He modelled himself on Degas as social observer – a man up to his eyeballs in the facts of glance, posture, gesture, dress and work. He was absorbed in the documentary role of painting. As Degas painted the Paris *café-concerts*, so he drew the London music-halls and was the first modern English artist to make a subject of popular culture. In the 30s he daringly began to use news photographs as a source for paintings, recreating on a large scale the smudgy images of Fleet Street: Edward VIII stepping from a State coach, or Amelia Earhart's landing in the rain at London airport.

Degas's nudes had a particular impact on Sickert – those late pastels of women cleaning and towelling themselves, unselfconscious as cats, watched by the artist-as-voyeur. *Je veux regarder par le trou de la serrure*, Degas told Sickert: 'I want to look through the keyhole.' When the facts of ordinary life dispelled the sacrosanct aura of the studio nude, one was left with a different kind of body – a *social* body, watched and used by others, in all its domesticity and indifference.

Degas taught Sickert to despise the 'ideal' nude; and Sickert brought this attitude to London, where it jolted English depictive painting and laid long consequences for the work of later painters, notably Freud and Auerbach. In England, Sickert argued, the conventions of the ideal nude had fostered 'art' without vulgarity and become an educational disaster. Naked bodies ought to be drawn in relation to clothed ones, as in the *Tempesta*, the *Déjeuner sur l'herbe* or Degas's whorehouse scenes; an all-nude composition, even by Ingres, suggested 'a dish of macaroni, something wriggling and distasteful'. Naked people were social and sexual beings, and their nakedness demanded the context of real rooms, real furniture, other people with their clothes on. For study, it was the *draped* figure that counted:

> I think all great and sane art tends to present the aspect of life in the sort of proportions in which we are generally made aware of it. I state the law clumsily, but it is a great

principle. Perhaps the chief source of pleasure in the aspect of a nude is that it is in the nature of a gleam — a gleam of light and warmth and life. And to appear thus, it must be set in surroundings of drapery or other contrasting surfaces . . .[28]

Sickert believed in ordinary subjects taken from common life. 'The plastic arts are gross arts, dealing joyously with gross material facts.'[29] Hence his two-figure interiors of 1903–10, which derive from Degas's brothel scenes: a man dressed, a woman naked. These, and most of all the 'Camden Town Murder' series of 1908-9, distressed English taste, which took such works as *L'Affaire de Camden Town*, 1909, as journalism and pornography.

Sickert *Nuit d'Eté* c. 1906

In their dense ribbed paint, these Sickerts describe a sexual world of Edwardian England: the curt randiness of a middle-class using the lower class as its brothel. John Addington Symonds, Sickert's friend, penned their verse equivalent:

> The little bedroom papered red
> The gas's faint malodorous light,
> And one beside me in the bed
> Who chatters, chatters half the night.

Auerbach felt 'an inborn sympathy with the social point of view from which [Sickert's] subject is viewed':

Helen Lessore wrote somewhere that [Sickert's locales] are grubby miserable bedrooms: well, those bedrooms with girls in them, where the sheets smell of human congress, they don't look in the least depressing to me — they seem to be really very jolly places. I recognize my life in those streets and in those bedrooms! I felt at home in Sickert's world. And a very enjoyable world it is, too! Those Mornington Crescent bedrooms, with plump sweaty nudes in beds, seem to me extremely desirable places to be in.

Sickert *L'Affaire de Camden Town* 1909

Auerbach has found quite a few people who could regularly put up with the taxing routine of sitting for him. His wife Julia, whom he first drew in 1959, has been posing for him regularly since 1976. Apart from her, there have been two constant models in his working life, people who became themes of his art in themselves. One is 'J.Y.M.', Juliet Yardley Mills, a professional model whom Auerbach met in 1957 when she was working at the Sidcup School of Art; she offered to pose for him privately and did so, often in continuous sessions of four or five hours at a stretch, through thick and thin, for more than thirty years. Over that time she became a close and permanent friend of Auerbach's, who has turned her into one of the most vivid personages in modern depictive art, transformed by repetition and re-seeing into a human icon as memorable as Giacometti's wife Annette or his brother Diego.

The other, her predecessor, 'E.O.W.', the model for most of Auerbach's nudes and female heads up to 1973, was Estella (Stella) West. They were lovers throughout the years over which Auerbach came to maturity. Their relationship was full of quarrels, intense (at least at first) and sometimes violent: 'I had nothing to lose; she had extreme courage, health and no sense of self-preservation.'[30] Stella West was fifteen years older than Auerbach, and in her he could piece together the broken security which is the orphan's burden; if anyone, early on, helped him to manage his sense of the world, it was Stella West. This would have deep effects on his art. His need for stability within the threatening flux of experience would be absorbed, through E.O.W.'s constant presence as a subject, into the very marrow of his painting and projected on his habits of work. Little by little, Auerbach's sublimated yearning for the lost figure of nurture would work its way out in fixed habits and, above all, in the belief that a chosen body or face could be inspected and painted *ad infinitum*, that each encounter binds you closer to it without losing its 'otherness' in the stagnancy of habitual response; in short, that no intimacy is altogether repetitious.

Colour Plates

1971~89

54 Head of E.O.W. – Profile 1972

55 Bacchus and Ariadne 1971

56 Spring Morning – Primrose Hill Study 1975

57 Looking Towards Mornington Crescent Station – Night 1973

58 Seated Figure with Arms Raised 1974

59 Rimbaud 1976

60 To the Studios 1977

61 Primrose Hill 1978

62 Study for St Pancras Steps 1978–79

63 Julia Sleeping 1978

64 J.Y.M. Seated V 1979

65 Head of Julia II 1980

66 Head of Michael Podro 1981

67 Head of Julia 1981

68 Head of J.Y.M. I 1981

69 Euston Steps 1981

70 Primrose Hill – Winter 1981–82

71 Portrait of Catherine Lampert 1981–82

72 Interior, Vincent Terrace II 1984

73 To the Studios 1983

74 To the Studios III 1983

75 Head of Debbie Ratcliff II 1983–84

76 Head of J.Y.M. II 1984–85

77 Reclining Head of J.Y.M. 1983–84

78 Tree on Primrose Hill 1986

79 Head of Jacob 1984–85

80 Head of Julia 1985

81 Head of J.Y.M. V 1986

82 Head of J.Y.M. II 1986

83 To the Studios 1985

84 From the Studios 1987

85 Head of J.Y.M. IV 1986

86 J.Y.M. Seated 1986–87

87 Head of Catherine Lampert 1986

88 Head of David Landau 1987

89 Julia 1987

90 J.Y.M. Seated 1987–88

91 Portrait of Catherine Lampert 1987

92 The Chimney – Mornington Crescent II 1988

93 Mornington Crescent – Night 1988–89

VIII

In 1948, when she and the seventeen-year-old Auerbach met, Stella West had no interest in art or art students. She was a stage-struck amateur actress of thirty-two, a handsome, feisty woman with a thick mane of blonde hair. Her husband had died leaving her 'very hard up', with three children to raise. She survived by running a lodging-house at 81 Earl's Court Road. One of her tenants, still indignantly remembered, was the future spy novelist Len Deighton: 'He used to take my coal without asking, and cook eels on my stove while I was out, so that the whole downstairs reeked.'[31]

Though an ideological innocent, Stella West had joined the little Communist Unity Theatre to get acting experience, unpaid. There, she found herself cast with Auerbach in a production by Frank Marcus of Peter Ustinov's *House of Regrets*. She played a White Russian landlady 'with all manner of funny lodgers', and to complete the loop between art and life the cast used to rehearse in her own lodging-house, where she met Auerbach for the first time. He had a walk-on part as a general's batman and delivered his one and only line in a thick *mittel*-European accent: 'Dostoyevsky vass a ghrreat writer.' Stella West liked him on sight. 'Frank was a very beautiful young man, looking very much older than his years, very mature. If he hadn't been a painter he would probably have been an actor. He looked more twenty-one than seventeen. I didn't think he was attracted to me. I thought I was much too old.' In this she was wrong. By the end of 1948 Auerbach, prompted by Herman Essinger, moved out of his digs in Hampstead (which were, in any case, inconveniently far away from the theatre and the art school) and into a basement room in the tall narrow house in Earl's Court Road. He and Stella became lovers. Their affair rapidly became inseparable from their working relationship as artist and model. 'I feel a little uncomfortable painting nudes of people when there is no physical relation', Auerbach now reflects:

> I think life drawing from the body of a stranger is a fine thing in an art school, but there's a real reason for recording someone whom one's close to. For one thing one knows exactly whether it's 'like' or not. For another, if the person has wakened one's mind, one knows what's not worthy of her, so one isn't going to pull any funny little tricks. Besides, if you're working with someone with whom you are involved, she may get fed up; you might quarrel; she may find it an intolerable burden and punish you by not sitting for you. The whole thing's got a totally different sort of tension from the simple transaction with a hired model.

For her part, Stella West remembers that the posing began as 'a sort of game', turned regular in the early 50s, became an unvarying routine after her children went off to boarding-school at Christ's Hospital in 1954, and became 'harder and harder as the years went by ... more demanding'. There was never a time when Auerbach was *not* a slow worker: *Head of E.O.W.*, 1955, took two years and three hundred sittings. Continuity was everything, and although Auerbach moved into his present studio in Camden Town in 1954 he always went to Earl's Court (and after 1961, when she moved out into the suburbs, to Brentford) to paint Stella. She had a job as a nurse in a Family Service Unit in the East End, and 'I used to come flying back to Earl's Court to Frank, who would be biting his nails and in a great temper if I was late. He would start on a charcoal drawing, scratching away and charcoal all over the place.' She realized that, despite the tyrannous demands of the schedule, and young Auerbach's way of getting 'terribly irritable', she was in a sense working *with* him and not just sitting there like a turnip. 'Yes, I felt a sense of collaboration, very much.'

It stayed with me . . . Sometimes I cried, sometimes Frank's painted me with tears streaming down my face because he seemed so cruel and so far removed from me, and I'd think: well, what am I? I'm nothing, nothing. But I was something . . . The first inkling I got of this was when I was sitting and thinking about my childhood, which wasn't easy. Suddenly Frank said to me, *Stop thinking that! Stop bloody thinking that!* And I realized there was some telepathy, some actual communication between us when he was painting me. It did matter to him, but he got terribly cross when I moved. Frank didn't want me to walk around; he didn't want me to even *look*, although I did sometimes. Mostly I looked at a spot on the wall, and he used to paint with the canvas propped on a wooden kitchen chair, because he had no easel in my place. Everything was all dripping with paint. Mostly we worked in my bedroom, because I could lie on the bed and so on, and the chair became more and more encrusted with paint, like a stalactite.

The routine never seemed to vary. Auerbach painted E.O.W. three nights a week. When he came round she would sit for two hours with one short break. On Saturdays she would put a joint of lamb in the oven downstairs and pose for an hour. Then a five-minute break, a look at the joint, and another hour's work. Then they would eat the lamb. For lack of an easel, Auerbach had to fall to his knees to get at the canvas on the chair: a strange tableau, the tyrannical youth kneeling in a bog of paint in front of E.O.W.'s pale ample body in the cramped bedroom, staring and muttering at her from five feet away. The physical impossibility of standing back and taking a distanced view of the body is inscribed in the heavy laborious surface of these early nudes. 'What used to distress me so much was all the scraping-down that he did. He used to scrape and scrape, every time. Of course the painting would be left with me, on the kitchen chair, and I would look at it – and then the next time he came round he'd destroy it, which sometimes made me feel I'd been wasting my time.'[32]

From 1956 to the end of 1958, however, Auerbach finished no more than two or three paintings and made only ten drawings he felt he could keep. His first show had left him with a sense of crisis; he had not realized how eccentric his paintings looked and how criticism would fasten on the thickness of their paint.

Somehow, I think, I had become conscious of what I looked like to the outside world – all the thick paint and so on; partly the fact that I had to adjust myself to doing a job, teaching two days and three evenings at art school. On Wednesdays I would work here during the day, teach at Bromley from 6.00 to 8.30, be given a lift back to the Earl's Court Road where Stella still lived, arrive about 9.00 and paint Stella for two hours before going to bed. I worked very hard.

One of the survivors, a *Head of E.O.W.*, 1957, is merely a profile bas-relief, the ochre globe of the head silhouetted on a brick-coloured ground, tender in feeling but inert. There is more animation and solidity in the two 1958 half-length nudes of E.O.W. with her arms crossed, in which her torso is vehemently rotated by the pull of the shadow cast by head and neck, and the highlight on the sloping pillowy breast; this effect is tentative in the first version but in the second, where the red hooking trace that indicates the shadow beneath the breast is clearer and the darkness on the face more pronounced, it acquires a tonal force that puts energy in the mud and gets the turgid webs of paint moving.

The drawings now began to be as ambitious as the paintings. Auerbach's hope to invest charcoal on paper with the density and 'presence' of paint was realized for the first time in a set of large heads done in 1956–57. They bear the scars of their making: so much rubbing and erasing that the paper wore through in spots that gave trouble, like the cranium of Kossoff, and had to be patched. But these drawings, mainly of E.O.W., have a disciplined amplitude of form which looks, in retrospect, quite singular; it is highly conscious of its methods – as in the triangular swipes of light that work as 'brushstrokes', cut from the charcoal with an eraser, to enclose Stella's face in an irregular kite-shaped frame – and yet instinctively drawn towards solidity, being swift, deep and ample. ('I have to begin with a lump in my mind.') It is the polar opposite of the Cubist fragmentation which, strung on a decorative grid, had become one of the conventions of English art in the mid-50s. The charcoal strives to integrate the features, to carry the form round the back of the head, out of sight. 'Nothing can be left out', he would say thirty years later, 'but you have to bury the irrelevant *in* the picture, somehow.'

94 E.O.W. Nude 1954

95 Half-Length Nude 1958

96 Head of E.O.W. 1955

97 Head of E.O.W. 1956

98 Head of E.O.W. 1956

99 Head of E.O.W. 1957

100 Head of Leon Kossoff 1957

101 Head of E.O.W. 1960

102 Head of E.O.W. I 1960

103 Head of Julia 1960

104 Seated Figure II 1961

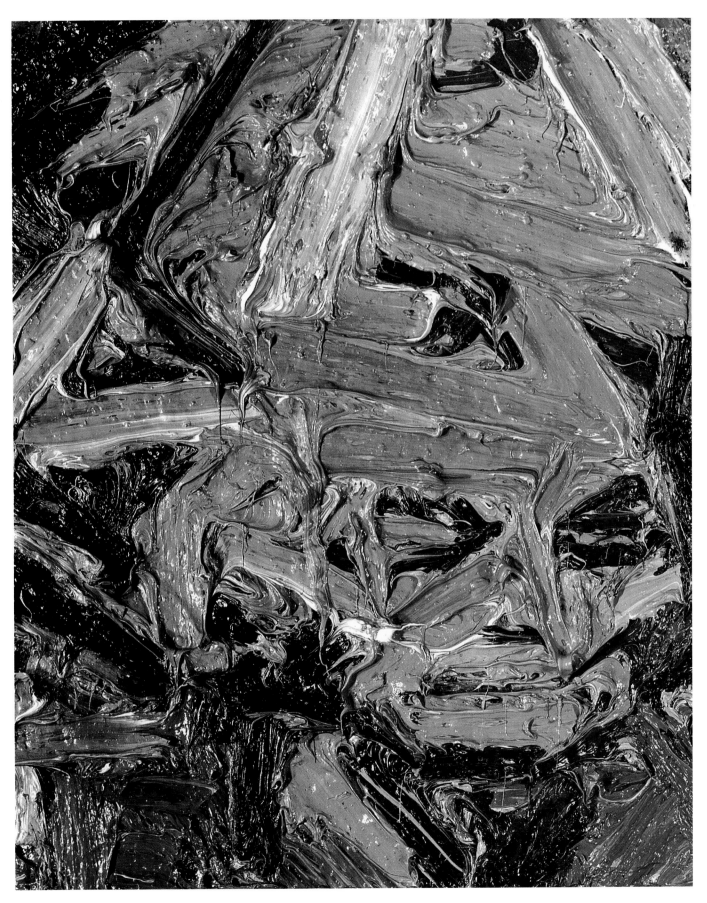

105 Head of E.O.W. 1967

106 Head of Gerda Boehm 1961

107 Head of Gerda Boehm II 1961

108 E.O.W., Nude on Bed 1959

To do this, he gradually realized, paint would have to relate to drawing in a different way. When a painting failed, it was usually because the paint-mass was laid over a conventional base of 'topographic' drawing – Euston Road realism with grotesque calluses. He must somehow integrate his growing sense of paint as an 'accumulating substance within which the whole world can be experienced'[33] with his need for patient and repetitive scrutiny. The key seemed to be wildness, so that the agenda of the painting stayed open until the last moment of its completion. 'Think about the vehemence that goes into some late Matisses – you get a radical reorganization at a very profound level at the very last stages.' He got Alfred Barr's book on Matisse in the early 60s and was impressed by its sequential photographs of the development of Matisse's *Pink Nude*, 1935. 'By the end it seems to reach an absolutely arbitrary stage where the charms of the earlier versions – and it must have been as charming as a Boucher – have gone. That sort of courage is independent of surface look . . . In a good painting *everything* is painted with the pressure of a grander agenda behind it, but sometimes the agenda isn't clear to the artist until the very end. It gives the secret unity, the general pressure [of experience] that gives life to this or that object. The problem is always to identify it. Then the act of recognizing it can burst the painting, and often it will.'

Colour alone, he realized, would not do that. His larger problem was to get the paint moving, to modify the sense of arrested time and slow deposit that was built into those interminably reworked surfaces – to give gestural energy to the lump.

One important catalyst had been the show of Abstract Expressionist paintings held at the Tate Gallery in 1958, which gave the artist, now twenty-seven, his first proper view of the New York School. Rothko was no use for his purposes: too static, a floating glow without mass. Pollock looked rather more to the point, but his continuous webs of improvised gesture finally seemed too generalized and unspecific, lacking in physical weight.

But de Kooning's work was another matter. It was clearly based on categories of figure and landscape, and its formal properties – the sense of edge and line, its concern with weight and definition of form, and its figure-ground contrasts – came out of an engagement with the Old Masters and a tradition of studio practice which Auerbach recognized at once. The Dutchman's hooking, rhythmic line evoked bodies in the jostle of elbow-forms and crotch-shapes, and drew them openly in the totemic *Women*. His paint surface was a membrane, now thick and now a wash, but always under some degree of torsion and tension from the boundaries of the forms. And the linear qualities of de Kooning's style were embedded in the swiping of the brush; the gesture and the form were one. At the same time there was enough contrast between figure and field in his work to give Auerbach's figural obsession a handle on it.

In sum, Auerbach found himself admiring in de Kooning what he admired in Soutine – the sort of draughtsmanship which is deeply painted, bathes shapes in air and carries the eye around the back of the form, rather than leaving it with the contours and colour of a flat patch. If any American artist of the 50s seemed to Auerbach to have matched the terms of Bomberg's 'spirit in the mass', that person was de Kooning. The example of Abstract Expressionist gesture did not wreak a sudden change in Auerbach's work, as it did in other English painters like Peter Lanyon and Alan Davie

Matisse *Pink Nude* 1935
(work in progress)

de Kooning *Woman I* 1950–52

149

at the end of the 50s, boosting them out of their Cubist framework. Instead it was slowly and cautiously absorbed, slowed down by the thickness of Auerbach's surface, which it energized in terms of vectors pushed through the paint – directional brushstrokes which wiped aside the clutter of *pentimenti* under the paint-skin. The first work in which this became clear was *Shell Building Site from the Thames*, 1959, a view down into the deep cut of the excavation for the skyscraper. The perspective of the floor of the hole, with the stumps of steel columns and the clay side rising to a high horizon line, dominated by the kite shape of a crane's raised booms, is done entirely with broad directional brushstrokes, furrowed and mucky but still insistently linear. It is spatially open and conveys a sense of air (or if not air, at least some variation of near-and-far substance). It is perhaps the first painting of Auerbach's that *seems* to have been done quickly, even though the look of speed is an illusion. Its scaffolding predicts the forceful drawing in sticks and bars of paint in his views of Primrose Hill and Mornington Crescent in the late 60s.

Shell Building Site is by no means his last big painting to be done in pure or near-monochrome; its lessons about framing a structure in air would be clarified in *Study after Deposition by Rembrandt II*, 1961, where the scaffolding of crosses in Rembrandt's painting in the National Gallery is thinned and schematized and the figures at the foot of the Cross are reduced to a lonely huddle of impastoed tan forms on a background the colour of cracked asphalt, a Baroque darkness – opaque space – that dominates the whole image. But from now on, Auerbach would tend to use monochrome as a way of testing the water when on the edge of a formal jump of some kind. Wanting to distance the image and give it air, he was insecure about colour: when, in *Nude on Bed II* and *Seated Figure II*, both 1961, he widened the field of view to include the space and furniture of the studio as a recognizable room, he worked in grey. These small paintings, along with the laconic scrunches of pigment that define E.O.W.'s body in *E.O.W.*,

Rembrandt *The Deposition*
or *The Lamentation over the Dead Christ*
1637–38 and early 1640s

109 Shell Building Site from the Festival Hall
1959

110 Shell Building Site from the Thames 1959

Nude lying on her Back, 1959, and *Nude on Bed III*, 1961, also mark the effect of Giacometti on Auerbach's work: distance, greyness, an 'impossible' gulf between the eye and the subject, and a feeling – especially in the latter painting – that the figure is threatened by the size of what is, in fact, a domestic space. This device of the looming wall, which had been present in Auerbach's work since the excavation streetscapes of the 50s (most dramatically in *Shell Building Site*) was his deduction from the backgrounds of Rembrandt and Caravaggio.

But the claims of colour could not be put off for ever. Around 1960 Auerbach began to enrich his earth, dun and grey palette. These, and flake white, had been the only pigments he could afford. But with his 'naive contract' with the Beaux-Arts Gallery – all his paintings for £1500 a year – he could buy expensive chromes and cadmiums without too much anxiety. This was just as well, for he was beginning to chafe against the limitations of a narrow palette. Thick plaques of paint in the colours of sand, stone or lead had to look like bas-relief sculpture, whether they were meant to or not. Perhaps colour would put their pictorial character back on top.

Between late 1960 and the summer of 1961 Auerbach made a set of frontal heads of E.O.W., all life-size or slightly larger. They keep the tonal structure of the charcoal drawings of her head, along with the emphatic diagonal vectors of shadow. But in *Head of E.O.W. I*, 1960, most of the work of extracting the form of her head from its bog of pink and buttercup-yellow pigment is done with discontinuous patches of cadmium red – a colour which became one of the main regulators of Auerbach's surfaces in the 60s. *Head of E.O.W. II*, 1961, though it uses the same yellows, reds and pinks, is more conventionally tonal, but there is more certainty in the paint-handling, the ploughed brushmark that delineates the bridge of the nose, the squeezed modelling of the right cheekbone and eye-socket. By keeping E.O.W.'s head to the right Auerbach was able to reduce its sculptural look; if centred, it would have been too like a formal bas-relief.

Several monochrome heads of E.O.W. follow, much wilder than the colour versions. Gestures push the mask to the limits of recognizability. The sculptural roundness of *Head of E.O.W. V*, 1961, is brusquely contradicted by two brushmarks that cut into the hair and brow from the surrounding grey ground. Two pendant dewlaps run from E.O.W.'s chin to her neck in version VI, 1961 – shapes which hold no discernible relation to her real face, and which would reach a grotesque extreme seven years later in the goblin-like yellow *Head of E.O.W. II*, 1968. In another grey painting from 1961 her left cheek is modelled, defaced almost, by a craggy blob of white which sticks out an inch from the already raised surface, and an irrational black brushstroke runs from the right eye-socket to the upper corner, as if venting the pressure below the surface. These are gestures of exasperation, signs of Auerbach's anxious will to openness. 'To work on a pre-ordained armature is a *sine qua non* of second-rate painting. The idea that one might not be free to make radical changes at the end of a work appals me. I don't think of the end as fine tuning – it's a radical change of channel.'

Painted by Auerbach on his knees in the upstairs bedroom, the images of this moment in his work have a strange devotional quality. An ejaculatory grandeur

struggles to break the cosiness of the domestic scene. In some ways they reiterate Rembrandt from far away, as Auerbach's painting of the hanging carcasses in the Smithfield Meat Market (the scene where he and Kossoff had drawn twelve years before) reconsiders Soutine. At about this time he also painted a small group of compositions with several figures, the most peculiar of which is *Gaumont Cinema, Camden Town*, 1963. In a mood of restlessness through that year Auerbach would break off work, walk down Mornington Crescent and pay his four shillings to see a movie at the Camden cinema. Though Auerbach is no *cinéaste* he went to the Gaumont 'fifty or sixty times', by his guess, usually walking out half an hour into the movie. He would go half an hour early, draw while the lights were on, and continue to scribble by the light of the screen after the projection started. He only stuck out one film — a B-grader about vampires, shot in Italy, directed by Roger Corman and starring Vincent Price. 'It was a great film and I watched it all the way through'; one of its images, a man in profile smoking a cigarette in close-up, is preserved on the blue screen of *Gaumont Cinema, Camden Town*. This painting, so reminiscent of Sickert's music-hall scenes in palette and eyeline (a view downwards into the stalls, from the left side of the loge), is the only reference to mass media in Auerbach's whole oeuvre. Why bother with this (for him) peculiar motif? Perhaps because its implied subject, the enthronement, as it were, of an image before a crowd of worshippers, connected with his museum experience of predellas, altarpieces and icons.

Gaumont Cinema was also his only attempt to paint a crowd — to poach, for a moment, on the territory of Kossoff, in whose company he continued to sketch in museums and in the street through the early 60s.

From now on the habit of working from a remembered motif, prompted by sketches, would become a steady part of Auerbach's routine, providing relief from the obsessive confrontation of the model in the studio. With her two daughters Sarah and Julia and her son Michael, Stella West had moved to Brentford, outside London and much further away than Earl's Court. Through the 60s, grumbling about the distance, Auerbach would arrive on the train three nights a week: 'He used to come on Saturday nights, and always we had cake', Stella West recalls:

> Sometimes Lucian Freud would come too. We had the Saturday Night Nosh. I used to put the joint in the oven, turn it low, and then model for him for a couple of hours, by which time the joint was done; sometimes my kids would bring their boyfriends; we had this big table in the room, Frank would sit at one end and I at the other, and it was wonderful. I was very happy in those years.

Stella West's parlour at Brentford is commemorated in one of his more Sickertian pictures, *The Sitting Room*, 1964, done in London from studies. It is a haven of warm putty-coloured light framed by dark red carpet, picture-rail and window-frame, whose heavy texture, as in Sickert's interiors, reinforces its feeling of intimacy and closeness; Christmas cards are on the mantelpiece, one of his own paintings (abandoned by him and rescued by Stella) hangs on the wall, and a lamp with a scalloped parchment shade — still the first piece of furniture one notices, twenty-five years later, in E.O.W.'s modest cottage outside Malvern — rises on a stalk that bisects the canvas. Stella West and her two daughters standing in the back garden at Brentford gave him the motif for his first paintings of groups rather than single figures: the two versions of *E.O.W., S.A.W. and J.J.W. in the Garden*, one finished in 1963 and the other in 1964. These ambitiously large paintings – more than six feet high, a size without precedent for Auerbach – seem to condense his struggle to push his work from stasis to movement, and from mass to linear structure, without losing its corporeal heft. In size, airiness and confident lock of structure, they are both in the *gran maniera*; but the differences are extreme. In the first, E.O.W.'s body is sculptural, as though carved from a single block of butter-coloured substance, head, arms, dress, legs and all. Planted on the ochre earth of the garden, she towers over her daughters in the background (one of them holding a black cat). She is protective, standing face-on, her pose reinforced by a clear cage of perspective lines: the garden fence, a crisscross of red trellis. Her rootedness is stressed by the paint strokes, level and horizontal, taking their cue from a bar of ochre light in the grey sky.

In the second version this monumental clarity is breaking up. Some linear elements of the background assert themselves more: one sees a greenhouse, outlined in red, and the steel frame of an unfinished high-rise to the right of E.O.W.'s head, and above it a licking, recurved line that represents the boom of a crane. But this linearity now invades the figures. Sarah and Julia West are still there, but hard to pick out among the welter of angles and hooks that fuse them to the background. And the *ur-mutter* trunk of Stella West is changed. The same red line of the background structures eats into it, unifying it with the background, flattening the space of the painting. The head becomes a rough gourd-shape, outlined in red. The security of the body's column wavers, like an image in a distorting funhouse mirror, or a figure reflected in water. One thinks for a moment of 60s de Kooning women, the floozies of the Accabonac ponds, half-dissolved by backlighting. But Auerbach had not seen these paintings in 1963 and this, in any case, is tougher and more structural. Every bounding line of E.O.W.'s figure is dense with pictorial purpose, and it is their energy, rather than the inertia of thick paint, that anchors her both to the picture plane and to the depicted earth of the little garden in Brentford.

Some smaller heads of E.O.W. from 1964 reflect Auerbach's search for a linear structure within the mass in a somewhat different way. Painted from life under electric light at night they turn the glare of a single light source into a violent agitation of paint depth: pure white pigment, piled inches thick, with black and ultramarine in its chinks. Strands of pigment straight from the tube – red, yellow, blue, sometimes not touched by the brush – worm their way across the surface, indicating the contours of brow or cheek. It is a weird conjuncture: a sense of light not far from Impressionism, combined with this heavy, convulsive surface.

The paintings that followed these, in 1965–66, were among the thickest Auerbach had ever done. Or to be precise, they give the strongest *impression* of depth, due to their small size and their isolation (in recessed box-frames, under glass) as ragged plaques of pigment: the proportion between the area of the image and its thickness was forced to the limit. Rather unexpectedly, this had the effect of slowing down the 'expressive' impact of the work. More illustratively recorded, the pose of *E.O.W. on her Blue Eiderdown II*, 1965, might strike one as full of pathos, the huddled body of a bare victim.

115 Head of E.O.W. II 1964

116 E.O.W., Head on her Pillow 1965

117 E.O.W. Sleeping II 1966

118 Head of E.O.W. 1964

119 Head of Gerda Boehm 1965

Hogarth *Shrimp Girl* after 1740

Manet *Berthe Morisot with a Bunch of Violets* 1872

But the density of the paint and the subtlety of its colour (arctic white flushed here and there with rose, on the surge of the pale blue quilt) delay one's empathy and objectify the forms. One does not think of its mass in a simple way as a symbol of agitation or obsession but rather, as David Sylvester once put it, 'as the vehicle of a vision of reality'.[34] This density can verge on the tragic, as in the 1965 *Head of Gerda Boehm*, but it is never pathetic. It gives the slanting, stacked forms of E.O.W.'s trunk and limbs a degree of emotional distance, while insisting on their physical reality. The lump of the body, reconstituted as paint, imposes itself. The eye feels the drag of its gravity. It seems as thick as mud and yet alive – a Golem, or a fragment of one. By now Auerbach's surfaces took to a further extreme the ambition Andrew Forge had described a few years earlier: they were a way of gambling with the image, 'coaxing or bullying features out of the vagaries of its surface . . . finding the most precise and delicate inflection of form, a foreshortened arm, a lost profile, couched in an impossible welter of matter that seems ready to flop off the canvas onto your shoes.'[35] Everything is curdled, air no less than substance. Sometimes the grain of the surface is so deep and cryptic that one can hardly decode the body at all. It takes some scrutiny to find the model's profile in *E.O.W.'s Reclining Head I (E.O.W., Head on her Pillow)*, 1965, though in a second version from 1966 it is quite clear, white on white again, lying there with the stony exhausted dignity of a tomb-figure on its catafalque. What clarified the game of hide-and-seek between the image and the physical stress of the paint was the colour, which in the early 60s attained a dramatic intensity: reds, pinks, Veronese greens and chromes.

This was colour right through, not tint lying on top of a bas-relief; the thickness of the paint seemed to push the colour out towards the eye. In the more restrained *E.O.W. on her Blue Eiderdown*, 1965, the coldness of the colour – the spectral white of E.O.W.'s body against the blue – is relieved by a narrow pink strip at the top left, a background of dark Indian red, and a cascade of pistachio green below the quilt. Perhaps the most remarkable thing about these paintings, apart from Auerbach's ability to suggest controlled formal equivalents for the body through the piling of paint – a simultaneous distance and intimacy, not the 'hot' lapel-grabbing involvement of Expressionist conventions – was the beauty and delicacy of these thick surfaces. The paint is peculiarly fresh. Its texture moves from deep parallel grooves to seemingly arbitrary channelling, from bosses or knots of pigment standing proud of the surface to the most delicate little tufts and hairs of drawn-out, toffee-like colour left overhanging the deeper strokes below. You know that a few extra runs of the brush through this sticky, vulnerable stuff would mash the colour and turn it into amateurish mud. The distinctness and vibrancy of colour declares the restraint of Auerbach's apparently violent touch. For all the labour that went into them, these thick paintings, at their best, have the immediacy of an oil sketch, even a watercolour: one begins to see why the spontaneity of Hogarth's *Shrimp Girl* and of certain Manet oil sketches, like that of Berthe Morisot, had the value of talismans for Auerbach. 'Thick, thin, what's the difference? The point is to push through to a certain directness.'

But the 'directness' is not sculptural. 'I have to begin with a lump in my mind' is one of Auerbach's tenets, and his instinctive idea of sculpture is a lump (something carved or modelled, like a Brancusi or a Rodin, rather than assembled from pieces, like a

González or a David Smith). That goes with his fixation on the haptic. A particular favourite of his is Rodin's *Iris* — the figure wildly spraddling, every inch of its surface mashed and squeezed. But Auerbach has never had the smallest desire to sculpt, partly, no doubt, because his haptic impulses are entirely absorbed by the thick paint, but mainly because the idea of making sculpture went against the grain of his art. Sculpture seemed more pre-determined than painting, less open to big changes at the last minute. 'I cannot conceive of a way of working in which you make an armature and then put things on it. It's exactly those decisions about size, gesture and so forth that one wants to leave until *last*.' No matter how thick they got, his paintings still did not want to be modelled sculpture.

Rodin *Iris c.* 1890–91

IX

He had to free his colour, and from 1965 onwards he did so through a sequence of landscapes, some of Mornington Crescent near his studio, others, fuller of nature, at Primrose Hill.

Townscape and landscape did not stare back. They did not require, as the model did, a mutual relationship. They were perhaps open to invention in a different way. You did not need to paint townscape devotionally. It fostered a different sort of curiosity. Certainly it allowed – in fact, demanded – a different way of working. Auerbach could not set his easel up *en plein air* and start working under the eyes of people in the street or the park in what he called 'the ludicrous way I *do* work'. Instead he made sketches outside, and worked up the painting from them in his studio. This, as it turned out, encouraged him to build a firmer structural grid for his paintings, derived from the observed and literal architecture of the city.

Meanwhile, under the influence of the more variegated colour of out-of-doors – the red of traffic-lights, green of awnings and yellow of signs, no less than the vaster and more subtle effects of natural light in the park – his colour opened out in a way that it might not have done had he kept it, and himself, indoors. He was freer to imagine colour; and this liberty would before long be fed back into the figures and faces.

There was nothing picturesque about the spot he chose. Its main merit was its proximity to Auerbach's studio, for, as he put it to Richard Cork,

> One starts a large painting, one has certain arbitrary habits or ambitions, and simply to make a record of . . . a decayed memory isn't sufficient. There has to be a conflict between what one wants and what actually exists; so one goes out and does a drawing, and it's always easier to do a drawing of a place nearby. Also there is a kind of intimacy and excitement and confidence that comes from inhabiting the painting and knowing exactly where everything is, and a sort of magic in conjuring up a *real* place, a record that is somewhere between one's feeling . . . and the appearance. Well, more than appearance. Substance![36]

The place is in north London – the three-way juncture of Camden High Street, Crowndale Road and Mornington Crescent, NW1. Coming out of Mornington Crescent tube station you see nothing but ordinary outer-city clutter: gooseneck street-lights, traffic-signals and metal Y-barriers laid over a background of fish-and-chip signs and off-track betting shops amid the roar and stink of traffic. Under that texture are Victorian remains, the seedy terraced curve of Mornington Crescent and one quite grand building, the Camden Palace Theatre, built in the 1880s with a green copper dome and two big arches like eyebrows, raised on pairs of engaged columns with tall plinths beneath them. Next to the station is a triangular plaza with a bronze man on a pedestal. If you dodge through the traffic and clamber over the railings you see that it is a statue of the Radical politician Richard Cobden, who in 1838 established the Anti-Corn Law League in Manchester and was, not incidentally, Sickert's father-in-law.

120 Behind Camden Town Station, Summer Evening 1966

It was given to the Vestry of St Pancras by a public subscription whose main contributor was Napoleon III. It looks forlorn. Next to it, surrounded by a black Victorian iron railing, is a stairway to some catacomb below street level, now blocked with a clutter of ferns, plastic rubbish and busted doors.

Not very inspiring, one would think. But Auerbach found in it a specific English character of chaos, dinginess and suggestiveness. This was the London that had never been painted. 'I haven't painted [Mornington Crescent] to ally myself with some Camden Town Group, but simply because I feel London is this raw thing . . . This extraordinary, marvellously unpainted city where whenever somebody tries to get something going they stop halfway through, and next to it something incongruous occurs . . . this higgledy-piggledy mess of a city.'[37]

The cityscapes are also construction sites. The structures they describe seem spiky, provisional. They are more like scaffolding than finished buildings, partly because some redevelopment was going on around Mornington Crescent in the mid-to-late 60s, but largely because of style: Auerbach's love of linear structure embedded in thick substance. But he was trying to complicate it. He was not looking at a hole in the ground but at a visual bustle that formed a maze of orthogonals. Hence the less successful ones look like conventional 'Euston Road' townscapes, full of scenographic detail – windows, gables, railings, a zebra crossing and stick-figures marching to and fro – but mired under the weight of paint. Pigment and space are better joined in the *cloisonné* effect of *Mornington Crescent with the Statue of Sickert's Father-in-Law*, 1966, with its red and black grids enclosing shards of ochre and more red, lit with five sharp streaks and one patch – no more – of lemon-yellow. But townscape, no less than landscape, means air and light, open space, not an indented wall of pigment. One can follow Auerbach's efforts to create a town-space that was less simply illustrational in two versions of the same view across Mornington Crescent. The first, *Mornington Crescent*, 1967, is

121 Behind Camden Town Station, Autumn Evening 1965

conventional in colour and makes its space by diagramming its recession in line, but the second, of the same title and date, creates space with two devices: a hot cadmium-yellow field that presses the foreground towards one's eye, and an equally emphatic upside-down v of black paint that drives one's gaze back to the vanishing-point. The pull between the two gives the painting its tension. In *Mornington Cresent IV*, 1967, he increased the illusion of depth with colour alone – a transparent silvery sky, a cold mild London light, which retains its impasto and is doubled in the rain-wet pavement below, while the oblong patches of red and blue that stand for railings and street-lights seem to dance within the grid.

In all, between 1966 and 1973 he painted sixteen images of this street-junction, and it was largely through the early ones that Auerbach's colour began to shake itself free from umber and ochre; while a more emphatic drawing, in deliberate straight bars, worked its way out. In some respects this was a Cubist grid, heavily modified by the impulse to gesture, as though Auerbach were looking for a diagrammatic form to replace the sheer mass of his pigment. Undoubtedly the example of Bomberg helped too: the linear scaffolding of his landscapes in Palestine closely anticipates Auerbach's own landscape drawings. But the main inspiration came not so much from Cubism itself as from the deductions made *from* Cubism (and Matisse) by the Russian–French artist Nicholas de Stael (1914–55), whose work Auerbach had seen at the Matthiessen Gallery in London in 1952. De Stael's paintings of the Midi from the early 50s were laid out in broad bands and patches of colour, with all lines thickened to bars and most shapes squared off into irregular oblongs, suavely but solidly modelled with a palette knife, abutted against or laid on top of one another without intermediary shading. Because each patch was so discrete and physically clear, the effect was comparable to that of a *papier collé* – more elegant than the excremental rawness of early Auerbach, but intriguing in their relations between thick paint and full-blown colour.

de Stael *Composition* 1950

122 Mornington Crescent 1967

123 Mornington Crescent, with the Statue of Sickert's Father-in-Law Cobden 1966

De Stael is echoed in *Studio with Figure on Bed II*, 1966. The title counts – 'studio *with* figure'; it is one of a group of interior paintings from 1966–68 in which the eye pulls back from the isolated figure or close-up head, seeing the body in ambient space, a thing among others – the planes of bed, floor, wall, mirror and a slender column with a T top that is the attenuated form of Auerbach's kerosene stove. J.Y.M. stretches out on the purple bedspread with the rectangular clutter of racks, picture frames and shelves rising above her. Her body is a spindly twist overlaid with gouts of red, subordinated to the main structural play of the image – the rectangles of red, purplish-blue and cream, stacked up in the flattened space. This architecture is clarified in the versions that follow – the same motif, the same contents of the room, their achieved differences reflecting Auerbach's belief that 'to have a different shape of canvas and to move a few feet to the right or left presents one with a totally different formal entity and it is just a new problem.'[38]

Finally one reaches the resolution of *Figure on a Bed*, 1968. Two-thirds of it is green floor, a richly worked Veronese green; its recession is stopped by the yellow and red surfaces of the bed, whose intensity seems to fold the upper third of the painting back towards the eye, so that the picture conveys not only the distance of the scrutinized object – J.Y.M.'s body, done in sticks of yellow brusquely articulated by black bars, raised on the crimson slab as though on top of an altar, an impression reinforced by the pale pillar-like form that the studio stove has become – but also its countervailing sensuous presence, displaced into the paint itself. Each stroke of the brush seems to have its particular weight and clarity, a direct outlet of feeling into substance, mark by decisive mark, the specificity of the touch grounded in the long-meditated concreteness of J.Y.M.'s presence in the artist's life, and in his occupation of this particular room. And yet in its sudden eloquence and brightness of colour the image *feels* like an apparition, a thing 'materialized' whole and entire, all at once. And as the critic Colin Wiggins remarked of this group of 1967–68 paintings, 'The apparent distortion of the figure invites comparison with Francis Bacon. Bacon's lying figures, however, always occupy an artificial stage which seems to have been coldly painted as an arena within which the act of painting is performed. Auerbach treats the space, the bed and the figure with an equal intensity. His figures consequently lack the theatrical segregation and isolation of Bacon's . . . *Figure on a Bed* is calm and ordered with the expressionist appearance external only.'[39]

This effect rose from a change in Auerbach's facture which had been on its way since the middle of the 60s and became pervasive by their end – the complete absorption of drawing into the painterly stroke, so that the form of a head or body, instead of growing by accretion into a solid mass, was improvised, laced together by its graphic energy. The paint is still thick, but no longer crusty, and the part of Auerbach's now clarified colour is to evoke its lost mass. E.O.W.'s reclining head, its icy nose thrusting up against its warm earthen background, is almost mummy-like, indifferently staring at nothing in particular, bound up in broad strips of white pigment, further articulated by slashes of black; the sense of an architecture of girding criss-cross marks, each bracing its neighbour against toppling into chaos, becomes acute in a slightly later yellow version from 1970. By now, E.O.W. looks shrivelled and crone-like, and a third version of her

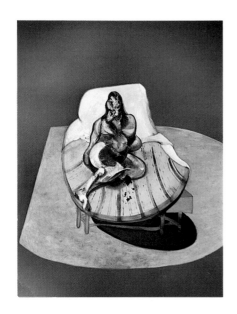

Bacon *Study for Portrait of Henrietta Moraes on Red Ground* 1964

reclining head seemed to the English critic Robert Melville to convey 'a rather frightening atmosphere of prediction', with the enigmatic letters HA scrawled into the paint by her head producing 'an atmosphere of ritual murder'.[40] That was too Expressionist a reading, though these heads of E.O.W. do suggest pathos, even desolation.

Taken together, Auerbach's portrait heads as the 60s turned into the 70s suggest a crisis of patience in him. They become grotesque, even caricatural. Though Auerbach kept saying, then as now, that the thrust of his drawing was towards tactile reality, it is hard to detect much of a realist impulse in the goblin that his habitual model becomes in *Head of E.O.W. II*, 1968 – a yellow slit-mouthed mask with one barbel hanging off the chin, the surges of paint suggesting an inner energy so wrenching that you expect her flesh to turn round, like that of the Irish hero Cuchulain, beneath her skin. A more caricatural graphic brusqueness pervades some small portraits of other models (Paula Eyles, Renée Fedden and Gerda Boehm) in 1969–71; their heads are shoved to absurdity by a jagged black outline. These are like latter-day reflections on the sombre, grotesque heads in the human pyramid that surges up in the foreground of Goya's *Pilgrimage to San Isidro*.

A similar impetuousness entered his landscapes of the park at Primrose Hill in the late 1960s. He had painted this scene occasionally before. But these embrowned, rather congested landscapes did not give much hint of what would happen when, in 1968, he began again. As in Mornington Crescent, he did not work direct from the motif; there was no way of adapting his cumbersome work-habits to the outdoors. Instead he made charcoal or felt-pen sketches of trees, horizon and clouds, scores of them, rapid notations not meant to be seen as developed drawings and painted from them in the studio. They were mere aide-memoires, he said, and they served only to evoke

> what it was like to actually draw there that morning . . . what I see is what I was looking at when I did the drawing and it reminds me of it. That's what it was for. I see the sunlight and the trees and the hill so I paint from these by looking at the drawing . . . I'm looking at black and white drawings and the lines signal colours to me.[41]

The pictures he worked up from these sketches were not simple extensions of them, any more than John Constable's fully achieved studio works – *Hadleigh Castle*, *Salisbury Cathedral from the Meadows*, or *The Leaping Horse* – were just 'elaborations' of his watercolours and cloud studies. In these studio pictures, which he rightly felt were the climax of his intentions, Constable had struggled to convey the freshness and density of nature while retaining a sense of occasion that transcended the passing moment, a security of pictorial utterance that would rival (and did, in fact, surpass) the architectural formality of Claude Lorraine. To judge Constable as though he were Monet is to misunderstand him; his sketches and cloud studies were marvels of clear, quick vision but the 'grand machines' were his masterpieces, his feats of pictorial integration. Perhaps only a twentieth-century taste formed by the Impressionist cult of the *plein-air* sketch could think otherwise.

124 Figure on a Bed II 1967

125 Figure on Bed 1968

126 E.O.W.'s Reclining Head 1969

127 E.O.W. Reclining 1970

128 Head of Gerda Boehm 1971

129 Head of E.O.W. II 1968

130 Head of Paula Eyles 1969

Goya *The Pilgrimage to San Isidro*
1820–23 (detail)

131 Head of Renée Fedden 1970

Constable *Salisbury Cathedral from the Meadows* 1831

Rembrandt *The Three Trees* 1643

Rubens *Autumn Landscape with View of Het Steen in the Early Morning* 1636

Constable *Hadleigh Castle* 1829

Auerbach's landscapes of Primrose Hill, from 1968 on, have something of this conscious striving towards a reflective grandeur of utterance. You might say that Constable was to him what Claude had been to Constable. In the landscapes, because they were *not* done from the motif, there was room for a mix of memory, experience and tradition somewhat different from Auerbach's sense of 'losing himself' before the live model. Prototypes in art came more to the fore and the memory of what he had studied in the museum modified his impressions of nature. At the same time, the influence of the living sitter dropped away: 'I think my sitters would tell you that I'm usually fairly abandoned when they're there, but there's a further degree of abandon when I'm doing the landscapes because I'm absolutely on my own.'

Auerbach's models of landscapes were mostly northern: the high skies and straight-scribed falls of shadow in Rembrandt's etchings, the tonal amplitude and rainbow-arched distances of Rubens, and *Road by a Ruin* by Philips Koninck which he copied several times. But his great exemplar was Constable, not because of his 'Englishness' – a debatable virtue – but because of his obstinacy and wildness: the ambition of his pictorial structure, the infatuation with paint, sticky and glittering, that pervades his late work, and the determination to butt through his experience of Claude to a way of landscape painting that had *not* begun on the Continent among the props of antiquity.

'I must go on', Constable wrote to his friend John Fisher in 1824. 'I imagine myself driving a nail. I have driven it some way – by persevering with this nail I may drive it home.'[42] (Grist, as one might suppose, to Auerbach's mill, there being few things he likes more in an artist than unreasonable doggedness.) The 'nail' in question was meant for the coffin of an idea upheld by most of Constable's English contemporaries, 'the seeming plausible arguments that subject makes the picture'.[43] And if it did not make the picture, what did? Nothing but paint, in its relation to what Lawrence Gowing called 'the momentum of the real'.[44] The attribute that makes Constable's *Hadleigh Castle* so unlike other paintings of its time is the significance Constable gives to the substance of paint as the regulator of pictorial feeling. We are not invited to see 'through' the pigment and, in construing it as a knob of rock or a marching bustle of clouds over the Thames estuary, keep the illusion while forgetting the stuff it is made of. The stuff remains obdurately there, both thick paste *and* air, light, earth, vegetation. In pursuit of 'notions of freshness – sparkle – brightness' Constable turned pigment itself into the substance of imaginative realization. The qualities of landscape are rolled back into the qualities of paint, its mounding and stickiness, its dilution and glazing, and in every bush and cloud one sees the medium undisguised at work, reconstituting the masses of landscape, the directional energies of wind and weather, and the scattered points of white light on a dewy field *in terms of itself*. This, and not just a correspondence of one artist's thick paint to another's, was why Constable became a talisman to Auerbach's work in landscape. Constable's direct touch is rhetorically exaggerated in Auerbach, though when it came to landscape Auerbach painted much more thinly than he had a few years before. His work by now took just as long to finish, not because of slow addition of layers, but because of ceaseless scraping off and beginning again. Picasso's dictum that 'a painting is the sum of its destructions' was, and still is, literally true of Auerbach, and nowhere more so than in his landscapes. A painting might take months but it would have to stay liquid right through to the end, which meant repainting it entirely every session. Though small by American standards (usually about fifty inches square) the landscapes were

[a] tremendous physical effort because . . . the way I work means putting up a whole image, and dismantling it and putting up another whole image, which is . . . physically extremely strenuous, and I don't think I've ever finished a landscape without a six or seven hour bout of work. Whereas, *a* person or *a* head is a single form and it can come about in a shorter period of time.[45]

Yet an undercurrent runs between the landscape and the nude as subjects. Just as Auerbach's nudes in the dark studio are signs for vitality – Sickert's 'gleam of light and warmth and life' in a dingy world – so the north London park, *rus in urbe*, is an oasis of exuberant nature in the midst of the city. However trampled the grass, muddy the paths or bare the dripping trees, it retains traces of Paradisical intent and Auerbach pounced on them, as if out to prove that one did not need to follow Matisse's and Derain's well-beaten track to the Mediterranean. In fact his first big pictures of Primrose Hill are literally primrose – as suffused with yellow as Arles or Collioure. One sees the sky first. *Primrose Hill, Summer 1968* is virtually a three-colour image, yellow, blue and red: the yellow making a single voluptuous field out of the sky and grass, tinged with green where it slabbers into blue underpainting; the blue driven in exclamatory zigzags across the sky, as though the girders and railings of Mornington Crescent had been tossed up and become the rudiments of cloud-architecture; in red on top of that, nearer the eye, suggesting trees. In such paintings, Auerbach had also come back close to some of David Bomberg's landscapes from Palestine, where a linear Cubist scaffolding describes the forms of Petra and Jerusalem. Their boldness and plasticity, the daring of construction and cancellation – as, for instance, in the zigzag of black strokes that shears through the grey sky of *Primrose Hill*, 1968 – retrieve the idea of landscape painting from the stagnancy into which it had fallen by the late 60s, where with a few exceptions (notably Richard Diebenkorn's *Ocean Parks*) it had become a mere appendage to abstraction, a ghost-image in the formalist machine. 'I do like a clear expression if I can get it – something that seems to lock like a theorem. And unless paintings have that kind of wit – unless underlying them there is a clear geometrical structure – I don't actually feel they work.'

Philips Koninck *Road by a Ruin* 1655

Bomberg *Jerusalem, looking to Mount Scopus* 1925

132 Primrose Hill, Winter 1961

133 Primrose Hill 1958

134 Primrose Hill, Summer Sunshine 1964

135 Primrose Hill, Winter 1962

136 Primrose Hill, Summer 1968

X

By 1968, as he was approaching forty, Auerbach's sense of his own range would seem to have locked tight: figures and portraits of known quantities in his life, the still-present E.O.W. and a new sitter, J.Y.M.; landscapes derived from long hard scrutiny, if not actually painted outside. The idea of doing allegories, mythologies or anything 'made up', seems quite out of synch with such a temperament; which may have been why, in a spirit of mingled perversity, homage and experiment, he decided to do it. He was persuaded by a most unusual English collector, David Wilkie. Wilkie was not rich; he worked in insurance; he lived in a small, neat suburban house outside London; he had bought, with passion and discernment, quantities of contemporary English art during the late 50s, including several Auerbachs. One of his more intriguing traits, to Auerbach, was his intense love of Titian, whose work – which Wilkie had seen in European museums during his army service at the end of the War – had converted a man who had never had any interest in art before into a devoted amateur. He wanted Auerbach to paint him a 'Titian'. Or perhaps two 'Titians'. He would not be put off. Auerbach had never done a commission (the portrait of Renée Fedden came later) in his life, but there was clearly something about Wilkie's obsession with Titian that intrigued him – a stubbornness, a will to reconstruct things from scratch, that chimed with his own character. After much discussion the two of them decided what the first 'Titian' would be: a version – which eventually became two versions – of *Tarquin and Lucretia*, in 1965. The one Wilkie wanted was not the work in the Fitzwilliam Museum at Cambridge, but a smaller painting he had seen in Vienna after the war, then given to Titian himself but today considered a school-piece. It takes in the upper half of the bodies, leaving out their legs and all except an indication of the bed. So Auerbach, who up to then had only painted one other composition from an existing work (the big 1961 version of Rembrandt's small *Lamentation* in the National Gallery), now found himself painting a portrait of a painting he had never seen.[46]

Studio of Titian *Tarquin and Lucretia c.* 1570

Studying a reproduction convinced Auerbach that 'Titian' had worked Lucretia from a reclining figure and then turned the painting on its side to make it a standing one. J.Y.M. posed accordingly (her posture, without Tarquin, can be seen reclining in some other Auerbach nudes of the time). The figure of Tarquin was improvised from a large drawing he made from the 'Titian' reproduction. Auerbach seems to pack the violence of the encounter into one thickly gouged stroke of paint that runs upwards from right to left and corresponds to Lucretia's arm, fending off the inexorable Tarquin whose upraised arm and dagger can be made out in the upper left corner. It reverses the modelling of 'Titian's' arm; 'Titian' made it soft and concave, Auerbach harsh and straight; we realize, after a moment, that consciously or not he is inducing us to see this central form as a wound, with suggestions of an abused vagina. As Richard Wollheim argued, 'we have . . . missed the wealth of Auerbach's transposition unless we see it as a comment on Titian's rendering of the human body *in extremis*.'[47]

If *Study after Titian II, Tarquin and Lucrece* is a reworking in the presence of a model of a painting Auerbach had not seen, his next 'Titian' project for Wilkie, *The Origin of the*

Great Bear, 1968, was an entirely invented version of a painting that did not exist – one that Titian might have painted but did not (although he painted two versions of a related subject, the condemnation of Callisto by Artemis). Titian would certainly have known the story from Ovid.[48]

Characteristically, Auerbach set the death of Callisto and her revival by Zeus as an eagle in a real landscape – not Primrose Hill this time but a view down the long slope of Hampstead Heath towards the city of London and South End Green; partly, perhaps, because of its associations with John Constable:

> However lax or non-existent was my study of the myth, I must have gone to Hampstead Heath one or two hundred times in the early morning, I used to see Michael Foot walking his dog, and look down on the ponds and on the Royal Free Hospital being built (on the right hand side – there is even a crane) and then scattered my mythological properties over the Heath: not entirely unfelt, and if *anyone* works long enough on *anything* inspiration occurs a bit.[49]

A little later he amended the last sentence:

> . . . when I wrote that if one went on long enough imagination occurred, I think I meant to say that a plastic study of the ingredients of the story produced its own poetry which would reflect back on the myth.
>
> I was looking at a Dutch genre painting yesterday, two women and a man making music and two dogs snarling at each other. I would lay a penny to a pound that some historian had suggested that the two dogs symbolized rivalry and jealousy between the women. Yet I have put two fighting dogs into a Primrose Hill picture simply because I saw them and they began to inhabit the picture; – this does not make the symbolical interpretation invalid.[50]

What David Wilkie got for his commission was a vigorous landscape drenched in springtime yellow, with a big flapping shape at the top left that is clearly Zeus in his aquiline form. The huddled, blackish-blue ideogram of Callisto's body lies on the grass below it, 'looking rather sweet', Auerbach now thinks, 'as did the bodies of dead soldiers to Siegfried Sassoon and Wilfred Owen'. A red spot next to her is Diana's hound, or possibly Michael Foot's. Diana herself, with her bow over her shoulder, is a red stick-figure partly concealed behind the reversed z of dark paint to the right. In the sky the seven stars of Ursa Major blaze forth. Such is Auerbach's version of the antique or mythological event in *cinquecento* costume – an actual landscape as the setting for a mythic occasion.

In 1971 Auerbach did another 'Titian' for David Wilkie, this time a free rendering of a work with which he was intimately familiar: the National Gallery's *Bacchus and Ariadne*, painted in 1522–23 for the Ferrarese duke Alfonso I.[51]

Worked up from drawings he made in the National Gallery, Auerbach's version is essentially a diagram of Titian's compositional vectors, with heightened colour. (As the critic Paul Overy remarked, it looks rather as though Bomberg's cubified Vorticist

Titian *Bacchus and Ariadne* 1522–23

stick-figures had been laid over one of his later Spanish landscapes from Ronda in the 30s.[52]) The suave orchestration of detail within the major forms has been, however respectfully, omitted. None of the figures are recognizable as themselves, and few even as figures, unless you use a postcard of the original as a crib. Then it becomes plain that Ariadne has not, in fact, vanished; the red of her sash has been transposed into a hooking gesture of the brush that stands in for her body and quite faithfully repeats its turning posture. The leopards are more like scribbled tom-cats and Bacchus has disappeared into a blackish-blue ideogram with a flurry of red strokes, the cloak, streaming away to the right. The Dionysiac revellers are hatched summarily in orange; Auerbach's attention was caught, but not long detained, by the rhyme between the round instrument and the face of the tambourine player; the satyr on the far right, and the torn-off animal haunch he brandishes like a club, are rendered in stick-posture. The most prominent and legible figure in Auerbach's version is neither Ariadne nor Bacchus but the god Pan, who robustly strides across Titian's foreground, wreathed in snakes.

Instead of being described in their bodies, Ariadne's encounter with Bacchus is abstracted – figured in the sky, as two sharp horizontal vs colliding along a linking axis. This echoes the cloud formations in the Titian, where a blade of white cloud runs from above Bacchus' head and penetrates the fluffier vapour above Ariadne's – a piece of subliminal symbolism of which Titian could scarcely have been unaware – but, in diagramming the god's tumultuous approach to the girl, it becomes an exercise in displacement. The feeling of Auerbach's painting has been shifted from figure to landscape; the vital colour of Titian's bodies, drained from Auerbach's version, is to some extent restored by the tumult of blues, yellows and greens that indicate foliage and sky; even the delicate ring of eight stars in the firmament above Ariadne's head gets magnified in his version to a heavy torus, like a rough sketch of one of Uccello's

139 Rimbaud II 1976–77

mazzocchi (Florentine hats), as pictorially emphatic as Ariadne, Bacchus or any of the rest of the cast.

The most eccentric paintings Auerbach made at Wilkie's prompting were two portraits of the poet Arthur Rimbaud. They were an exception to Auerbach's work-habits, being entirely 'made up' from photographs. Rimbaud (1854–91) was the arch-example of precocious genius and instability of character for the Symbolists at the turn of the century – the *poète maudit* who, having transformed the expectations of modernist poetry as a teenager with 'Le Bateau ivre' (1871) and the fragmentary 'Une Saison en enfer' (1873), vanished to the Middle East, renounced writing altogether, became a gun-runner in Ethiopia and died wretchedly in a Marseilles hospital from cancer of the leg, aged thirty-seven. The side of Auerbach that loved craziness and fixation loved Rimbaud, of course: but the tribute remains a peculiar one. The boy rebel against Catholicism, the homosexual occultist, is elevated in all his bony ginger-haired glory (the source being a photograph of Rimbaud at seventeen) into nothing less than the altar of the Cornaro Chapel in S. Maria Vittoria in Rome, normally occupied by Bernini's *Ecstasy of St Teresa*. Wilkie had originally asked Auerbach to 'do' a version of the Bernini, but 'I think he envisaged a model posing on a sort of mound in the studio – this seemed impracticable, and I saw no point in working from a photograph.' The patron then came back with another idea: what about a portrait of Rimbaud? At this point Auerbach, presumably with Sickert's photo-derived paintings in mind, thought he could go the whole hog and combine the two – 'rather', he wrote with a poker face some years later, 'like the man in *Pickwick Papers* who wrote an article on Chinese metaphysics by looking up first "China" and then "metaphysics" in the encyclopaedia, and then "combining his information" . . . the image, in a batty way, made a sort of sense.'[53]

Rimbaud at 17, from the cover of *Illuminations*

Bernini *Ecstasy of St Teresa* 1645–52

140 Seated Model III 1963

XI

When Auerbach was studying at the Royal College of Art, he met Julia Wolstenholme, a fellow-student from Yorkshire. They married at the beginning of 1958 and their son Jake was born in the same year. The marriage was not, at first, a success; indeed, it was a fiasco. They drifted apart, without divorcing, and did not get back together again until 1976. Since then Julia Auerbach has been the subject of a warm and intimate series of portraits, and Jake Auerbach — now a television producer — has also been painted and drawn.

141 Seated Figure with Arms Raised 1973–74

142 Seated Model with Arms Raised 1973

But Auerbach's main model from 1963 onwards was Juliet Yardley Mills, whose presence comes to pervade Auerbach's figure painting in the later 60s, as E.O.W.'s gradually moves out; Auerbach finished his last head of Stella West in 1973. 'J.Y.M.' is not *named* in any of his picture titles until 1970, when Auerbach scrawled her initials on a portrait — a gesture made, he said, 'for the same reason that you carve people's names on trees. . . . one writes the name of the person or people that one is in love with.'[54]

Velázquez *Sebastián de Morra* (the dwarf) 1644

That she is a different model, evoking different feelings, is clear right from the start. She first appears in 1963: a slender, long-legged woman sitting in a chair in the Camden Town studio. Her pose does not have the weight, the inward-turning and massive expression of E.O.W.'s usual postures. Her arms are up behind her head, like a cat stretching, thrusting her breasts forward from the arched axis of her spine. Her head tilts back. Drawing this body in its double-trapezoid frame of the chair's back and legs, Auerbach's line breaks and blots into harsh excited gestures. He would paint the architecture of J.Y.M.'s habitual pose, the head framed in the upraised arms and the neck supported on linked fingers behind, over and over again — at one point in 1973 he associated it with Velázquez' portrait of the dwarf Don Sebastián de Morra and did

several versions of J.Y.M. sitting on the bed with her legs pointing, very foreshortened, straight towards him. And in the seventy or more seated portraits and close-up head studies of J.Y.M. that he would paint over the next twenty years, she always returns the painter's gaze: there is a look – head cocked back, sometimes seen a little from below, a bit quizzical, sometimes challenging – that makes them quite recognizable as a series, aspect after aspect of a mutable character with whom Auerbach was intensely engaged. Whereas, the portraits of E.O.W. do not usually look back at you, and when they do, never with the same briskness: that would not have been right for Auerbach's *dea mater*.

E.O.W. was still very much there, of course: a constant model, but now an aging one, like Auerbach's cousin Gerda Boehm, who also continued to pose for him through the 1970s. In Auerbach's closing portraits of E.O.W., made in 1972–73, the *145* strong face is looking remote and rather weary; she is playing the role of the Older Woman in a drama that is winding down. E.O.W.'s presence had lost its power to provoke scrutiny and summon form. *Finita la commedia*. In the last portrait of all, E.O.W. is nearly cancelled into an expressionless wraith, the eyes mere splotches, the mouth annulled by a swipe of blackish umber that runs from mid-chin to beneath her ear. It looks curiously ill-considered, this image, as though he had been in a rush to get rid of it. The end of their long affair was acrimonious; it came in 1973 when Auerbach refused to take her to Italy with him, on his own brief and somewhat reluctant visit to Milan for a show at the Galleria Bergamini. He turned forty-two that year, and she fifty-seven. Given the intensity of their earlier relationship, and the length of their work together as painter and model, there could have been no way back; an artist paints a person n times, but not $n + 1$, because although the amount of reality contained in that head or body may seem inexhaustible and continue to do so for years, no gaze is really insatiable. Auerbach's paintings of E.O.W. had begun, twenty years before, in a spirit of devotional accretion, a slow obsessed layering. Her replacement by J.Y.M. confirmed and accelerated, though it did not directly cause, the freedom and comparative wildness of his mature style, whose main point (apart from a deepened expressive role for colour) was to get the whole surface moving under the action of drawing, the decisive linear marks of the brush in liquid paint.

143 Head of J.Y.M. 1970

144 Head of J.Y.M. 1972

145 Head of E.O.W. 1972

146 Head of E.O.W. 1973

147 Head of E.O.W. 1972

148 Head of Brigid 1973–74

149 Head of Michael Podro 1976

150 Head of C.D. II 1977

151 Head of Ken Garland 1977–78

152 Head of Catherine Lampert VI 1980

153 J.Y.M. Seated III 1981

154 Head of Margaret Schuelein 1983

155 Head of J.Y.M. 1984

156 Head of J.Y.M. 1986

157 Head of Catherine Lampert 1985–86

158 Head of Julia II 1986

159 Head of Julia 1989

160 J.Y.M. 1988–89

XII

By the early 1970s Auerbach's drawing and his painting were no longer independent of one another. His drawing had always reinforced his painting, and usually preceded it as a way of studying E.O.W.'s head and body; but in the early stages of his career you could not say that Auerbach's graphic work with charcoal or etching needle *looked* like his paintings. He could do things with line that he could not manage in paint. Auerbach was never comfortable painting a body with articulate volumes in any kind of action. (The figures walking in his streets and landscapes were stick-effigies, mere diagrams in motion.) Drawing is a 'lighter' and more experimental medium than painting, hospitable to the untried thought. Consequently the developments in Auerbach's drawings often preceded those in his paintings. The first clear sign of this was in the charcoal heads of E.O.W. from 1956–57, which pointed the way to the gradual mobilization of the surface of Auerbach's paintings. But there would be others, and the freedom with which Auerbach learned to handle the single brushstroke as a form-making gesture, after the 1960s, came out of constant charcoal drawing.

Of course, no drawing could possibly mimic the thick surface of Auerbach's early work. It is true that, for him – as for any other artist – both drawing and painting are records of an activity that unfolds in time. An essential part of the effect of early Auerbachs like the Cincinnati *Head of E.O.W.* is their time-bound quality: deposit after deposit of paint, silted there on the surface, gravelly and static, left by three hundred sittings. But though the paint implies time – and reinforces it by suggesting an antique head, an archaic fragment – nobody can disentangle from this substance the order and sequence of its arrival there. Finished painting tends to cover its traces. Whereas drawing, in its apparent impulsiveness, seems more open: scanning it, you can guess at the sequence of the network of marks (however partially) and enter the story of its construction. A finished painting may not tell you how it was finished; a drawing nearly always will. This is why drawing seems, though it may not actually be, a more 'intimate' medium than painting. It offers a narrative of perception, the gaze probing at the object, the hand converting its messages into marks, with a directness which is resolved and sublimated in the finished painting. And since this directness is the *sine qua non* of what Auerbach thinks of as 'raw' visual truth, it became urgent for him to narrow down the gap between drawing and painting. This was not a planned decision – no artist foresees the ends of his work in that way – but it shows clearly in his work's movement from opacity to clarity, from impaction and encrustation to a more gesticular surface; from the mass encountered in the dark to structures of light and colour. For drawing is what turns mass into structure and holds its parts firm, tensely imagined in all their disparities and linkages.

'Drawing is not a mysterious activity', wrote Leon Kossoff:

Drawing is making an image which expresses commitment and involvement. This only comes about after seemingly endless activity before the model or subject, *rejecting time and time again ideas which are possible to preconceive* [my italics]. And, . . . it is always beginning again, making new images, destroying images that lie, discarding images that are dead. The only true guide in this search is the special relationship the artist has with the person or landscape from which he is working.[55]

Auerbach does not just 'draw' for the sake of making interesting marks; he must draw *something*, an external subject, say the head (of E.O.W., J.Y.M., Gerda Boehm, Catherine Lampert, Sandra Kitaj, David Landau, Michael Podro) scrutinized for the nth time in the studio. Each of these nominal subjects has a welter of physical characteristics so complicated, and so interlocked, as to defy verbal summary, from the general set of the head's ball on the neck's stalk, to the relation of the nose to the cheekbones, the way the gaze streams from the recess of the eye's orbit, the lay and crinkle of hair, the shadow that hooks under the cheekbone, the surfaces that seem flat and frontal, the others that recede and carry the eye round the back of the head – a vast anthology of particular and minute differences, underlaid by the artist's own relationship with the sitter as a person, overlaid by the expressions that, even in immobility, flicker across the 'fixed' structure of his or her face. The permutations that present themselves to the artist's gaze are infinite, although they may not all be communicable, or equally 'interesting'. But one realizes that there is, at least, no reason why an artist should not draw the same head a hundred times. It is the variety that can be extracted from constancy, one image at a time, that counts, not some parade of made-up differences. But the significance of drawing *as a process* lies in the fact that, in the course of drawing the motif or nominal subject, another subject of drawing appears. This is the actual subject. It lies in the relation of one mark to another, not the general address of all marks to the motif: *disegno interno*, the expressive internal relations of drawing, the 'harmony', as distinct from *disegno esterno*, fidelity to likeness. The 'second subject' of drawing is drawing itself, its energies and tensions, its ability to move one's eye from one

161 Head of Gerda Boehm II 1978–79

162 Head of Gerda Boehm 1978–79

node of form to another, to make the gaze appreciate lines and areas of grey as signs of force and displacement as well as literal shadow or physical edge. But for these to manifest themselves with real power they must always be moving towards *this* head, *that* landscape, and so be keyed into the resistances of the real world. If mere likeness to the sitter or the tree in the park were the only goal, every drawing would be foreseeable and, assuming a certain level of skill on the artist's part, hardly worth finishing — a story whose telling cannot but bore the artist, since 'to do something predicted doesn't seem to me to be worth doing at all.' If the internal relationships of the drawing were all that counted, its address to the real world would be merely theatrical, a matter of convenience and mystification. Somewhere between the two, Auerbach's 'rawness' is sought and, with luck and persistence, found. Such a process of drawing was imagined by Samuel Beckett, in a paragraph addressed to his friend the Israeli artist Avigdor Arikha which applies just as well to Auerbach:

> Siege again laid to the impregnable without. Eye and hand fevering after the unself. By the hand it unceasingly changes the eye unceasingly changed. Back and forth the gaze beating against unseeable and unmakeable. Truce for a space and the marks of what it is to be and be in face of. These deep marks to show.[56]

'Deep' the marks may be, but the continuous reworking that builds up the surface of a painting destroys that of a drawing. No matter how long Auerbach takes to finish a drawing — weeks, usually — what one sees on the paper at the end is always the work of one day's session and one only. But each day's work is left overnight, taken up the next day when the sitter arrives, and then scrubbed back to a grey blur — usually to the sitter's disappointment, since there seems to be no end to all this. The work begins again. There may be fifteen, twenty, thirty vanished states in the end, each corresponding to a *giornata*, a day's work. Their only final record is the deepened, tarnished-silver surface the paper has taken on from so many coats of ingrained charcoal left by the successive erasures. After a while the paper sometimes wears away under the scratchy attack of the charcoal and the rubbing of the rag, and must be repaired. Hence the patches that infest Auerbach's graphic work. The glued-on paper has no formal intention, and no claim to aesthetic interest, as collage. Its edges do not relate to the action of lines and tones in the drawing — though this action *is* related, often very tautly so, to the edges of the original sheet itself. The patch is just stuff over a hole, brusquely put there by forced necessity. So why not throw the sheet away and start with a new white one? Because (or so Auerbach apparently feels) the ghosts of erased images 'in' the sheet contribute some pressure to the final version, which he is loath to lose. The patches were more common twenty years ago, when the only paper Auerbach could afford was thinner. Today he uses the heaviest Arches 'Not' surface paper, a plaque the thickness of deer-hide, which can stand more abuse. But it only comes in one size, and since he likes a squarish format for his drawings he has taken to gluing a half-sheet to a whole sheet, leaving a seam across the surface, usually across the sitter's face. This, too, has no formal intent. It is not meant to call attention to the 'materiality' of the paper as paper; or to set up a geometrical undertext, like the abutting of canvases in a Brice Marden. It is just a brusque compromise with what can be got.

163 Portrait of Sandra 1973–74

164–203 Drawing in progress for Portrait of Sandra 1973–74

Drawing seems lighter to him than painting – as it ought to, given his arduous and messy way of working with pigments. 'It seems to me much more intelligent to have a piece of black chalk in one's hand, to have a piece of paper, to be able to make one's points economically. I am delighted occasionally to be able to do that. [But] after a time it seems an impoverished activity, a sort of escape, and one gets back to painting.'[57] For Auerbach, the capacity for repeated attack that drawing demands is an index of maturity. 'When did Picasso grow up?' he once asked, in a moment of gaily shameless self-projection. 'With the portrait of Gertrude Stein, of course – so many sittings, scribbling at a piece of mud.' Forty-one work sessions went into *Portrait of Sandra*, 1973–74, and the drawing in progress was photographed at the end of each day on its easel. One sees it changing, not little by little, but radically – not like a time-lapse film of a plant growing, in which the unfolding of structure follows an irreversible and organic logic of maturation, but in fits and starts. The whole structure is redone each time, the notation going from a soft and almost flattering *sfumato* to clawing zigzag strokes of the charcoal [3] and then back again to near-blankness [6]; shapes, such as a narrow rhombus made by the contour of the shoulders and the inner shadow of the sharp collarbones, become dominant [7] and then are repressed [9], only to come back again as halves of themselves [12, 13], disappear once more [15] and reassert themselves in exasperated complication [23]; sometimes the high-cheekboned face is as beautiful as it would be to a photographer's lens [12, 15], but a few states later it has become as twisted as a False Face mask [17], only to turn into a ravaged patch of tissue with emblematic features, or a virtual blank. The final version does not look any more *like* Sandra Kitaj than a dozen of its erased predecessors, but it has the density that comes of exhausting most of the other alternatives – none of which are exactly 'given', though all inventions are forced by the pressure of fact: this woman in this chair in this room. 'I can do something that looks like one of my drawings in half an hour – but I find it unsatisfactory; it never seems specific enough for me, it never seems to be new enough. So I find myself going on . . . and as I go on I find the problem more and more impossible, and because, I suppose, of my temperament I find myself behaving in an excessive way in order to solve the problem.'[58]

In painting, the 'excessive' behaviour had come to mean redoing the picture each day *alla prima* until it came right. If it did not come right, Auerbach would scrape it all off and begin again. This caused an even more prodigal wastage of paint than he had allowed himself in his earlier work; dolloped out by the pound onto the table that serves for a palette, most of it ended up on the floor after a brief sojourn on the canvas. 'Almost all the paintings that I am not ashamed of have gone on for a painfully long time', but the results were now different – fluidity replaced the old encrustation.[59] There are very few *pentimenti* in Auerbach's paintings after the mid-70s, because the whole image tends to have been finished in one session. Sometimes, impatiently, he will leave the parallel tracks of scraping to speak for themselves as form, with their accidental marbling of the earliest layer of pigment caught in the weave of the canvas, as in the background of *J.Y.M. Seated IV*, 1979. But more usually the repainting is entire and, as Catherine Lampert put it, 'the oil paint . . . never disavows the look it had within the pot.'[60] On the canvas it has become kinetic – glisteny and driven, a machinery of strokes rather than

204 J.Y.M. Seated IV 1979

an array of patches. The eye, in reading them, is never still; the brushmarks hectically urge it along, along the contours and round the back of forms. There are, however, certain memories of the Old Masters involved in this, of Rembrandt in particular. Just as, in drawing, Auerbach's branching line contains overt semi-conscious references to those sudden hooks of the ink-laden nib which were one of the most often imitated aspects of Rembrandt's drawing style, so in painting the embedded bars of pigment left by the broad square brush are deeply influenced by Rembrandt's habit of modelling in explicit facets, each a daub of pigment squarely turned towards the eye. The structure of Rembrandts like *Portrait of Hendrickje Stoffels*, which Auerbach often drew in the National Gallery, finds its way into his own half-length portraits; the long leaning rectangles of her robe, building and driving into a diagonal movement that runs from lower right to upper left of the trapezoidal block of her figure, are metabolized into the long strokes that summarize the arms and torso of such paintings as *Portrait of J.Y.M. Seated*, 1976.

The search for marks that conveyed an unarguably physical sense of the motif, transposing its felt presence into the tactility of paint, would often force Auerbach's paintings to exaggeration. There was one angle on J.Y.M.'s head, tilted back and slightly to one side, resting against the chair-back, that he repeatedly painted in the 70s and 80s – not because it was a 'formal problem' that he needed to resolve, but because he had no choice about it; it was one of the ways in which J.Y.M. repeatedly sat. One sees him nagging at the broad intractable plane that runs from the ear to the cheek and reflects so much light. At first this plane makes the head look bucolic and almost fungal, something yellow rising on its stalk of brushmarks from the red shoulders. In a later version it recedes into a bandage-like structure of marks; then it swells out again, like a goitre, its protrusion exaggerated by the U-hook of dark paint scribed around it and echoed by two smaller Us – one for the ear, the other, presumably, a lock of hair – above.

205 Head of J.Y.M. 1973–74

206 Head of J.Y.M. 1974

There is a quality akin to desperation about these attempts to seize the excessively physical; one senses it, too, in the way the power of gravity – squeezing a face down into the coverlet – is conveyed in some of the reclining heads.

Uprightness gets its dose of exaggeration as well, to reflect a defiant frankness in J.Y.M.'s bearing. Auerbach had always been drawn to the pose which is the archetype of portraiture: the sitter exactly head-on and level to the painter, so that gaze meets gaze down a narrow cone of space. But, in fact, very few of his earlier portraits – especially not those of E.O.W. – do look back; the head turns, the eyes drop down slightly or break away, a reluctance to engage which reinforces the head's nature as an object and suppresses its use as a *tête d'expression*. (Probably this muteness reflects little more than studio fatigue over the long passages of time spent posing.) With J.Y.M., Auerbach felt able to risk a more direct engagement. It comes with the superb 1981 *Head of J.Y.M. I*: the sitter rearing up, not recoiling, but with her back, one is made to feel, pressed against the back of the chair; the hair resolved into a dense supporting architecture by the broad ochre-to-umber swipes of the brush on the right of the neck, and the returning gaze emphasized by the irrational swing of a mark around her right cheekbone, which both destabilizes the face by slippage and reinforces it through its relation to the free marks below. J.Y.M. is an imposing presence here, very old, almost hieratic. Yet although one has a strong sense of confrontation with the sitter, she has no recognizable facial expression and the eyes are virtually suppressed: the right eye as a black hollow within the orbit, the left one merged in paint except for a small gleam of red, like the reflection from a fox's eye caught in a headlight. The face-to-face pose demands engagement. Because of the lack of expression, the vehement marks with which Auerbach tries to summon up the density of her presence also push the image towards abstraction. But there it will not go, so that one's reading of it oscillates, rarely definable as a 'personality' but always strong as a 'presence', while Auerbach's gouts and swathes of paint struggle

Rembrandt *Portrait of Hendrickje Stoffels* 1659

207 Reclining Head of J.Y.M. 1974–75

208 Reclining Head of J.Y.M. 1975

209 Portrait of J.Y.M. Seated 1976

with the task of finding haptic equivalents for physical form. Sometimes one does, indeed, seem to be looking at a character. But in others, like *Head of J.Y.M. IV*, 1986, the pictorial scrunching and squeezing blots out all interest in recognizability and the whole face – except for the trace of a snout-like nose and a shadow under the eyebrows that breaks away into two cancelling gouts of greyed-down Venetian red – is subordinated to the glare of light.

Throughout such work, the sense of mass in movement is what counts. Auerbach was quite specific about that: painting must 'awaken a sense of physicality', transcend its inherent flatness, or fail. This was the exact opposite of that masterwork of academic American criticism in the 60s and 70s, the Greenberg Sanitation Scheme (held more rigidly by the acolytes than by the teacher himself) whereby Modernism was supposed to move in a continuous ecstasy of self-criticism, under the sign of a purified, non-depictive flatness, towards the point where everything not essential to it had been purged. Auerbach believed in no such scheme of art history, past, present or to come. Matisse's *découpages* were always cited as authority for it, but to Auerbach they meant something quite different:

> 'A late Matisse paper cut-out which seems on the surface, and perhaps to superficial or uninstructed viewers to be a decorative pattern . . . works, because it's a shape made from a sense of mass, rather than a shape made from a sense of shape, and a disposition made from a sense of infinite space, rather than disposition on a flat surface. I think there's a real barrier between the sort of painter who is arranging things on the surface for their own sake and the sort of painter who has a permanent sense of the tangible world.'[61]

The sense of mass and of deep space remained as basic to Auerbach's thinking in the 70s and 80s as it had ever been. Perhaps more so; now that the sculptural thickness of the

210 Head of J.Y.M. III 1985

211 Head of J.Y.M. – Profile IV 1987

212 Head of J.Y.M. III 1980

paint was gone, and the space around the subject less congealed and planar, it was the stroke itself that ran forward and backward and around, creating a sense of plasticity and turning. In the process, his reliance on stick- and girder-like shapes as drawn scaffolding disappeared, replaced by more fluid drawing. What this indicated was a growing mastery of touch. There was, certainly, a particular 'signature' in the marks: a preference for hooked closing shapes and Y-shaped open ones, a branching of cranked lines, which grew directly out of the earlier junctures of his drawing. You could not call it a stylistic device: it was more a natural frequency, the form unconsciously reached for in the act of converting sights to marks. But this fresh continuity of stroke, by clearing more air for improvisation, opened his work to a sort of lyrical imprudence. *Head of Julia II*, 1980, one of Auerbach's most masterful portraits, is also nearly absurd; the effigy that rises from its swirls, shags and hairy little peaks of paint, jostling and overlaying one another, is put within an inch of theatricality by the brown topknot of hair and the profile lines of the familiar curved chair-back, which, notched and twiggy, look for a moment like a masquer's head-dress. But once this impertinent reading is repressed, the head rises up once more with the solemnity of a rock in a storm. The dignity of Auerbach's stoniest portraits of E.O.W. remains, without loss, in the heads he would paint thirty years later. Images like *Head of J.Y.M. III*, 1980, or some of the heads of Debbie Ratcliff from 1983–84 seem inviolable in their succinctness and apartness, in the sonority of their dark colour, and in the discipline with which impassioned gesture is resolved as structure rather than wasted as surface rhetoric. The difference is that now the order is more complicated. The painter is fishing in deeper waters – a more disturbed flux of appearances, a more declared sense of the frustrations of spatial difference that rise between the painter's body and the other's, frustrations that must somehow be made sense of on the place that lies between, part barrier and part window, the flat white canvas.

213 Head of Charlotte Podro 1982

214 Portrait of Debbie Ratcliff 1983–84

215 Portrait of Debbie Ratcliff III 1984

216 Head of Catherine Lampert 1984–85

217 Head of Julia II 1985

218 Head of David Landau 1988–89

This project was also apparent in his landscapes. By the mid-70s he was 'tired of these angular geometries which I've dealt with and tried to supersede . . . I've drawn the clouds and there are certain massy, turning, pillowy, featherbeddy convolutions of earth and sky that have seemed to me a stimulus to try to get an image that extends my repertoire.'[62] In *Primrose Hill*, 1978, the clear division of earth and sky is almost suppressed; we seem to be in a cave, fairly churning with autumnal colours – ochres and oranges, Spanish reds, teetering patches of dark Hooker's green, which suggest the ripened density of English landscape in a way that bears homage to Constable. The human figures on the path and the red squiggle of a dog, beneath some poles and a scratch of telephone wire, look tiny in the midst of all this energy. The rhythmic unity between earth and sky is prolonged in other park landscapes of the late 70s and early 80s, whose compass of forms moves with ease between grand events in the sky – like the bulging lobe of yellow, edged in greeny-black, that shoves its way into the top of *Primrose Hill*, 1980 – and smaller incidents: rays of light, the bend in a path, railings, dogs, a woman with a pushchair, a running child. On a visit to Tretire in Herefordshire in 1975, he had got interested in a solitary tree, of which he made several drawings. This motif stayed with him, and back in London he continued to draw sketches of a lone hawthorn tree on Primrose Hill, the *donnée* of several paintings. This not-quite centred structure seems to surge out of the earth, spreading a canopy that holds up the wild sky; in its materiality and protectiveness it bears a distant family resemblance to Courbet's 'historic tree', *The Oak of Vercingetorix*, 1864.

Auerbach's last changes of townscape subject came in the 80s. At first glimpse *The Chimney – Mornington Crescent II*, 1988, suggests a Roman scene – Piazza Navona with the obelisk reared on Bernini's vaulting stone grotto, in front of the facade of St Agnese. But in fact this obelisk is only an incinerator chimney near the Mornington Crescent intersection, and the 'Roman' effect comes from the amplitude of the painting itself: the

Courbet *The Oak of Vercingetorix* or *The Oak at Flagey* 1864

219 Summer – Tretire 1975

220 Tree at Tretire 1975

221 Primrose Hill 1980

222 Primrose Hill Study – Autumn Evening 1979

vertical lancing the sky, into whose golden-ochre depths Auerbach's brush has scribed one broad arc, as confidently placed as the rainbow quadrant in Constable's *Salisbury Cathedral from the Meadows*. This scale of utterance has nothing to do with scenography, or picturesqueness. It is about painting as a ramification of life – the power of painting to make you concede that things you did not think mattered actually do matter. In the early 80s, when Auerbach produced a number of versions of the view from the pavement in front of the gate that leads to his studio in Camden Town, he was looking at an even less 'interesting' sight, if possible, than that of the Mornington Crescent intersection. The most ardent preservationist could hardly find much to love in this fragment of London: a spindly looking Victorian villa with a high narrow entrance on the left, to the right the stained concrete of some 60s flats with pseudo-modernist scoops on their facade – a speculator's vague memory of Oscar Niemeyer in the midst of Camden Town – and an alley in between. Nor could it be said that Auerbach turns this sight into a glimpse of the New Jerusalem. But in *To the Studios III*, 1983, the elements of the scene are taken up with a dashing effusiveness, broadened, recomposed; the angles of perspective sharpen to pull the eye into deep interstitial space, mullions become girders, the dingy glass of one round window blooms with gold, blue and reflected hatchings of Indian red, and in the sky the brush does its deep scribble of blue, a movement that seems about to break away from appearances and yet encompasses them in an ecstatic burst.

This ability to transform without romanticizing is, among other things, what 'maturity' means to a painter. In his own maturity, Auerbach's work suggests a way – only one of several, no doubt, but certainly one – out of the morass of ambivalence and coarsened self-reflexiveness in which so much of the art of the last twenty years has foundered. It reminds us that painting may still connect us to the whole body of the world, being more than just a conduit for debate about novelty, cultural signs and stylistic relations: that the shallowness, the vacuous proliferation of footnotes, to which the tyranny of art history has condemned it in the names first of avant-gardism and then of post-modernism, can be revoked if a painter or sculptor is determined to play a deeper and more direct game. What counts most in Auerbach's work is the sense it projects of the immediacy of experience – not through the facile rush of most neo-expressionist painting, but in a way that is deeply meditated, impacted with cultural memories and desires which do not condescend to the secondhand discourse of quotation. Like all painting, good or bad, it is coded. Because codes have origins and histories, it subsumes the artist's experience of other art. But the clear purpose of its codes is to clarify Auerbach's struggle, not to 'express himself', but to stabilize and define the terms of his relations to the real, resistant and experienced world: which is what art must do, today as yesterday, if it is to be more than chatter.

223 Euston Steps – Study 1980–81

224, 225 Two pages of sketches for To the Studios 1985

226 To the Studios 1985 (*see also col. pl. 83*)

227 Mornington Crescent – Early Morning 1989–90

228 Chimney in Mornington Crescent – Early Morning 1988–89

Auerbach's studio, 1985

Notes

List of Illustrations

Notes

All conversations with Auerbach are taken from taped conversations between me and the artist, February 1986 – January 1987, unless otherwise noted.

1. Frank Auerbach, 'Fragments from a Conversation', in *An Anthology from 'X'*, Oxford, 1988, pp. 23–5.

2. Catherine Lampert, 'A Conversation with Frank Auerbach', interview in *Frank Auerbach*, exh. cat., Arts Council, Hayward Gallery, London, 1978, p. 22.

3. *The Times*, 3 March 1971.

4. Lampert, 'A Conversation,', *op. cit.*, p. 22.

5. For the record: 'Michelangelo, Rembrandt, Gaudier-Brzeska, Soutine, Ruysdael, Gericault, Turner, Constable, Hogarth, Kossoff, Fragonard, Giacometti, Tintoretto, Titian, Cimabue, Picasso, Matisse, Léger, Poussin, David, Ingres, Delacroix, Cézanne, Goya, Vermeer, Derain, Manet, Monet, Courbet, Daumier, Piranesi, Piazzetta, de Kooning, Albert Pinkham Ryder, Mondrian, Bomberg, Matthew Smith, Sickert, Rubens, Koninck, Veronese, Tiepolo, Dürer, Rodin, Aztec and Egyptian sculpture, African art, Brancusi, Bacon, Velázquez, Gainsborough, Whistler, Corot, Vuillard . . .' Paul Bonaventura, 'Annaherung an Frank Auerbach', in *Frank Auerbach*, exh. cat., Kunstverein, Hamburg, 1986.

6. Lampert, 'A Conversation', *op. cit.*, p. 10. The correct title of the Dürer is *Conrat Verkell*.

7. Frank Auerbach, interview with Richard Cork, unpublished MS supplied by Auerbach, undated, p. 2.

8. See especially David Sylvester, 'Young English Painting', *The Listener*, 12 Jan. 1956: 'Auerbach . . . has given us, at the age of twenty-four . . . the most exciting and impressive one-man show by an English painter since Francis Bacon's in 1949. . . . These paintings reveal the qualities that make for greatness in a painter – fearlessness; a profound originality; a total absorption in what obsesses him; and above all, a certain authority and gravity in his forms and colours.'

9. Stuart Morgan, *Vogue*, May 1986.

10. Andrew Forge, 'Auerbach and Paolozzi', *New Statesman*, 13 Sept. 1963.

11. Frank Auerbach, letter to me, 1 Aug. 1988.

12. Lampert, 'A Conversation', *op. cit.*, p. 10.

13. Michael Roemer, interview with me, May 1987.

14. Richard Cork, *David Bomberg*, New Haven and London, 1987, p. 29.

15. Peter Fuller, 'David Bomberg: Pre-Raphaelitism and Beyond', *Art Monthly*, no. 107 (June 1987), pp. 3–7.

16. Michael Roemer, 'Frank Auerbach and Leon Kossoff', unpublished MS of lecture notes, undated.

17. Cited by William C. Lipke, preface, in Richard Cork, *David Bomberg, 1890–1957: Paintings and Drawings*, exh. cat., Tate Gallery, London, 1988.

18. Auerbach, interview with Cork, *op. cit.*, p. 8.

19. *Ibid.*, p. 7.

20. Lampert, 'A Conversation', *op. cit.*, p. 14.

21. Andrew Forge, introduction, *Helen Lessore and the Beaux-Arts Gallery*, exh. cat., Marlborough Fine Art, London, Feb. 1968, p. 12.

22. See John Russell, 'Colourmen', *The Sunday Times*, 15 Jan. 1956; Stephen Bone, *Manchester Guardian*, 11 Jan. 1956; Anon, *The Times*, 13 Jan. 1956; Sylvester, 'Young English Painting', *op. cit*; Helen Lessore, letter, *The Times*, 3 Feb. 1956.

23. Sylvester, 'Young English Painting', *op. cit.*

24. Leon Kossoff, 'The paintings of Frank Auerbach', *Frank Auerbach*, exh. cat., Arts Council, Hayward Gallery, London, 1978, p. 9.

25. Forge, 'Auerbach and Paolozzi', *op. cit.*

26. Leon Kossoff, introduction, *Leon Kossoff: Recent Paintings and Drawings, January – February 1973*, exh. cat., Fischer Fine Art, London, 1973, p. 5.

27. Auerbach, interview with Cork, *op. cit.*, p. 4.

28. Walter Sickert, 'A Stone Ginger', in *A Free House*, London, 1947, pp. 324–7.

29. Walter Sickert, 'Idealism', *Art News*, 12 May 1910.

30. Frank Auerbach, letter to me, 19 May 1988.

31. Estella West, interview with me, Feb. 1986.

32. *Ibid.*

33. John Russell, 'Millais: how art avenged success', *The Sunday Times*, 15 Jan. 1967.

34. David Sylvester, 'Nameless Structures', *New Statesman*, 21 April 1961.

35. Forge, 'Auerbach and Paolozzi', *op. cit.*

36. Auerbach, interview with Cork, *op. cit.*, p. 1.

37. Frank Auerbach, interview with Judith Bumpus, *Art and Artists* (June 1986), p. 27.

38. Catherine Lampert, 'Frank Auerbach', introduction, *Frank Auerbach*, exh. cat., The British Council, XLII Venice Biennale, 1986, p. 11.

39. Colin Wiggins, 'Frank Auerbach', *Artscribe*, no. 22 (April 1980).

40. Robert Melville, 'Poons and Custard', *New Statesman*, 22 Jan. 1971.

41. Lampert, 'Frank Auerbach', *op. cit.*, p. 9.

42. Constable to Fisher, 1824; cited in Michael Rosenthal, *Constable*, London, 1987, p. 154.

43. *Ibid.*

44. Lawrence Gowing, 'The Modern Vision', in Robert C. Cafritz, Gowing and David Rosand, *Places of Delight: The Pastoral Landscape*, Washington, D.C., New York and London, 1988, p. 226.

45. Lampert, 'A Conversation', *op. cit.*, p. 13.

46. Lucretia, the wife of Tarquinius Collatinus, was raped by Sextus, the son of Tarquinius Superbus, the last king of Rome, in the 6th century B C. Overcome with virtuous shame, she stabbed herself to death. Legend claims that this outrage led to Junius Brutus's revolt and the fall of the Tarquin dynasty. Virtuous Lucretia enters literature through Livy and Ovid's *Fasti*, going thence to St Augustine, Chaucer (*The Legend of Good Women*) and Shakespeare's *The Rape of Lucrece*.

47. Richard Wollheim, 'Titian and Auerbach', *The Listener*, 4 Oct. 1973.

48. Ovid, *Metamorphoses*, 2: 405ff. Callisto, an Arcadian nymph, was loved by Zeus and bore him a son, Arcas, from whose name 'Arcadia' derives. Her unchastity angered the goddess Artemis or Diana, the virgin huntress, who turned her into a she-bear. Time passed, and one day Arcas, a hunter now grown to manhood, met his lost mother in her ursine form on the slopes of Mt Lycaeon. Seeing only a bear, he pursued her into the sacred precinct of Zeus Lycaeus, a sacrilege punishable by death. Here, wandering with her dogs, Diana saw Callisto and killed her with an arrow. But Zeus intervened; swooping down in the form of an eagle he revived Callisto and carried both her and Arcas off into the heavens, where he remains as the star Arcturus and she as the constellation Ursa Major, the Great Bear.

49. Frank Auerbach, letter to me, 16 Oct. 1988.

50. Auerbach, letter to me, 20 Oct. 1988.

51. Ariadne, in the well-known myth, was the daughter of Minos, King of Crete. Her lover, the hero Theseus, had penetrated the labyrinth Minos built to imprison the Minotaur, killing the bull-man and returning through the maze with the help of a thread given him by Ariadne. Together, they fled to Naxos to escape Minos's rage; and there, after a short idyll, Theseus abandoned her and sailed away. Titian depicted the moment when jilted Ariadne, wandering on the shore, is found by Bacchus, who later marries her: resigned to death, she finds new life in the god.

52. Paul Overy, 'In the Footsteps of Titian', *The Times*, 16 Oct. 1973.

53. Auerbach, letter to me, 19 May 1988.

54. Lampert, 'A Conversation', *op. cit.*, p. 16.

55. Kossoff, 'The paintings of Frank Auerbach', *op. cit.*, p. 9.

56. Samuel Beckett, in *Avigdor Arikha*, London, 1986, p. 10.

57. Auerbach, interview with Cork, *op. cit.*, p. 5.

58. *Ibid.*, p. 2.

59. *Ibid.*, p. 3.

60. Lampert, 'Frank Auerbach', *op. cit.*, p. 7.

61. Lampert, 'A Conversation', *op. cit.*, p. 19.

62. *Ibid.*, p. 11.

List of Illustrations

Measurements are in inches before centimetres, height before width

1   Portrait of Robert Hughes 1986
    chalk and charcoal on paper
    $34\frac{1}{4} \times 30\frac{1}{8}$, 87×76.5
    inscribed, signed and dated lower right
    Private collection, New York

2   St Pancras Steps 1978–79
    oil on canvas
    $66\frac{1}{4} \times 54$, 168.3×137.2
    Rochdale Art Gallery

3   Birth, Marriage, Death 1951
    oil on hardboard on board
    $48 \times 72\frac{1}{4}$, 121.9×183.5
    signed and dated lower left
    Private collection

4   Summer Building Site 1952
    oil on canvas
    30×42, 76.2×106.7
    Saatchi Collection, London

5   E.O.W. Nude 1953–54
    oil on canvas
    $20 \times 30\frac{1}{4}$, 50.8×76.8
    Tate Gallery, London

6   Head of Leon Kossoff 1954
    oil on board
    24×24, 61×61
    David Roemer

7   Head of E.O.W. 1955
    oil on canvas
    15×12, 38.1×30.5
    Private collection

8   Head of E.O.W. 1954
    oil on canvas
    $15\frac{3}{4} \times 11\frac{3}{4}$, 40×29.8
    Private collection

9   Head of E.O.W. 1957
oil on canvas
20 × 16, 50.8 × 40.6
Ruth Roemer

10   E.O.W., Half-length Nude 1958
oil on board
30 × 20, 76.2 × 50.8
Private collection

11   Oxford Street Building Site II 1959–61
oil on canvas
84 × 66$\frac{1}{8}$, 213.4 × 168
National Gallery of Victoria, Melbourne,
Felton Bequest 1961

12   Head of E.O.W. II 1961
oil on board
19 × 14, 48.2 × 35.5
David Roemer

13   Study after Deposition by Rembrandt II 1961
oil on board
71 × 48, 180.3 × 121.9
Private collection

14   Nude on Bed II 1961
oil on board
20$\frac{1}{4}$ × 20$\frac{1}{4}$, 51.4 × 51.4
Collection R. B. Kitaj

15   Head of E.O.W. VI 1961
oil on board
23$\frac{1}{2}$ × 22, 59.7 × 55.9
Scottish National Gallery of Modern Art, Edinburgh

16   Head of E.O.W. V 1961
oil on board
24 × 20, 61 × 50.8
Private collection on loan to Tate Gallery, London

17   Smithfield Meat Market 1962
oil on board
72 × 60, 182.9 × 152.4
Ivor Braka Limited, London

18   View from Primrose Hill 1963
oil on board
48 × 60, 121.9 × 152.4
Australian National Gallery, Canberra

19   Head of Gerda Boehm II 1963
oil on double board
24 × 24, 61 × 61
Private collection

20   E.O.W. on her Blue Eiderdown VI 1963
oil on canvas
17$\frac{1}{4}$ × 20, 43.8 × 50.8
Private collection

21   Gaumont Cinema, Camden Town 1963
oil on board
35 × 57$\frac{1}{2}$, 89 × 146
Private collection

22   The Sitting Room 1964
oil on board
50$\frac{1}{4}$ × 50$\frac{1}{4}$, 127.6 × 127.6
Tate Gallery, London

23   E.O.W., S.A.W. and J.J.W. in the Garden I 1963
oil on board
75 × 60, 190.5 × 152.4
Private collection

24   E.O.W., S.A.W. and J.J.W. in the Garden II 1964
oil on canvas
75 × 60, 190.5 × 152.4
Private collection

25 Head of E.O.W. III 1963–64
oil on board
27 × 22¾, 68.6 × 57.7
Saatchi Collection, London

26 Seated Model in Studio IV 1964
oil on board
12 × 6, 30.5 × 15.2
Private collection

27 Portrait of Helen Gillespie I 1964
oil on board
29½ × 24½, 75 × 62.2
Collection R. B. Kitaj

28 Study after Titian II, Tarquin and Lucrece 1965
oil on canvas
26 × 24, 66 × 61
Private collection

29 E.O.W. on her Blue Eiderdown II 1965
oil on board
23½ × 32, 59.7 × 81.3
Private collection

30 E.O.W. on her Blue Eiderdown 1965
oil on board
18 × 24, 45.7 × 61
Private collection, New York

31 E.O.W., Head on her Pillow III 1966
oil on board
24 × 23½, 61 × 59.7
Private collection

32 Studio with Figure on Bed II 1966
oil on canvas
35½ × 27½, 90.2 × 69.8
Private collection

33 Reclining Figure in the Studio 1966
oil on canvas
24½ × 30, 62.2 × 76.2
Private collection

34 E.O.W. Sleeping 1966
oil on board
16 × 24, 40.6 × 61
Private collection

35 Mornington Crescent IV 1967
oil on board
45 × 55, 114.3 × 139.7
Private collection

36 Mornington Crescent 1967
oil on board
48 × 58, 121.9 × 147.3
Metropolitan Museum, New York

37 Head of Miss Steinberg 1967
oil on canvas
30 × 28¼, 76.2 × 71.8
Private collection

38 Figure on a Bed 1968
oil on board
40 × 30, 101.6 × 76.2
Private collection

39 Primrose Hill 1968
oil on board
48 × 57½, 121.9 × 146
Tate Gallery, London

40 Primrose Hill, Autumn Morning 1968
oil on board
48 × 48, 121.9 × 121.9
Private collection

41   The Origin of the Great Bear 1968
      oil on board
      45 × 55, 114.3 × 139.7
      Private collection

42   Mornington Crescent – Winter 1969
      oil on board
      45 × 55¼, 114.3 × 140.3
      Private collection

43   E.O.W. Reclining 1970
      oil on board
      21¾ × 24, 55.3 × 61
      Private collection

44   Seated Man 1950
      oil on canvas
      32¼ × 24¼, 81.9 × 61.6
      signed and dated upper left
      Private collection

45   Woman with Hands Clasped on Head 1951
      charcoal on paper
      30 × 22, 76.2 × 55.9
      signed and dated
      Private collection

46   E.O.W. Nude 1952
      oil on canvas
      30 × 20, 76.2 × 50.8
      Private collection

47   Portrait of Leon Kossoff 1951
      charcoal on paper
      30 × 22, 76.2 × 55.9
      signed lower left
      Jonathan Roemer

48   Head of E.O.W. 1953
      oil on board
      24 × 13¾, 61 × 35
      Private collection

49   Head of Leon Kossoff 1954
      oil on canvas
      24 × 20, 61 × 50.8
      Private collection

50   St Pancras Building Site, Summer 1954
      oil on board
      40½ × 50½, 103 × 128.3
      Private collection

51   Oxford Street Building Site I 1959–60
      oil on board
      78 × 60½, 198.1 × 153.6
      Tate Gallery, London

52   St Paul's Building Site c. 1955
      oil on board
      31¾ × 47⅝, 80.6 × 121
      Ivor Braka Limited, London

53   Maples Demolition 1960
      oil on board
      58 × 60, 147.3 × 152.4
      Leeds City Art Galleries

54   Head of E.O.W. – Profile 1972
      oil on board
      20 × 17½, 50.8 × 44.5
      Private collection

55   Bacchus and Ariadne 1971
      oil on board
      40 × 50, 101.6 × 127
      Private collection

56 Spring Morning – Primrose Hill Study 1975
oil on board
42 × 54, 106.7 × 137.2
Private collection

57 Looking Towards Mornington Crescent Station
Night 1973
oil on board
48 × 48, 121.9 × 121.9
Graves Art Gallery, Sheffield

58 Seated Figure with Arms Raised 1974
oil on board
20 × 20, 50.8 × 50.8
Arts Council Collection

59 Rimbaud 1976
oil on canvas
42 × 42, 106.7 × 106.7
Private collection

60 To the Studios 1977
oil on board
48 × 54, 121.9 × 137.2
Private collection

61 Primrose Hill 1978
oil on board
45 × 60, 114.3 × 152.4
Private collection

62 Study for St Pancras Steps 1978–79
oil on board
54 × 48, 137.2 × 121.9
Private collection

63 Julia Sleeping 1978
oil on board
$15\frac{1}{4}$ × 15, 38.8 × 38.1
Private collection

64 J.Y.M. Seated V 1979
oil on board
22 × 20, 55.9 × 50.8
Private collection

65 Head of Julia II 1980
oil on board
20 × 22, 50.8 × 55.9
Private collection

66 Head of Michael Podro 1981
oil on board
13 × 11, 33 × 28
Private collection

67 Head of Julia 1981
chalk and charcoal on paper
$30\frac{1}{2}$ × $22\frac{3}{4}$, 77.5 × 57.7
inscribed at base
Private collection

68 Head of J.Y.M. I 1981
oil on board
$22\frac{1}{8}$ × 20, 56 × 50.8
Southampton Art Gallery

69 Euston Steps 1981
oil on board
40 × 50, 101.6 × 127
Private collection

70 Primrose Hill – Winter 1981–82
oil on board
48 × 60, 121.9 × 152.4
Private collection

71 Portrait of Catherine Lampert 1981–82
oil on board
$28\frac{1}{8}$ × $24\frac{1}{8}$, 71.4 × 61.3
Private collection

72 Interior, Vincent Terrace II 1984
    oil on canvas
    48 × 52½, 121.9 × 133.4
    Private collection

73 To the Studios 1983
    oil on canvas
    54 × 47¾, 137.2 × 121.3
    Private collection

74 To the Studios III 1983
    oil on canvas
    42¼ × 50⅜, 107.3 × 128
    Private collection, New York

75 Head of Debbie Ratcliff II 1983–84
    oil on canvas
    26 × 26, 66 × 66
    Private collection

76 Head of J.Y.M. II 1984–85
    oil on canvas
    26 × 24, 66 × 61
    inscribed lower right
    Private collection

77 Reclining Head of J.Y.M. 1983–84
    oil on canvas
    26¼ × 28⅛, 66.7 × 71.4
    Private collection

78 Tree on Primrose Hill 1986
    oil on board
    48 × 54, 121.9 × 137.1
    Private collection

79 Head of Jacob 1984–85
    charcoal on paper
    34 × 27⅝, 86.4 × 70.2
    signed and dated lower right
    Collection R. B. Kitaj

80 Head of Julia 1985
    oil on canvas
    26 × 26, 66 × 66
    Private collection, New York

81 Head of J.Y.M. V 1986
    oil on canvas
    26 × 26, 66 × 66
    Private collection

82 Head of J.Y.M. II 1986
    oil on canvas
    28 × 24¼, 71.1 × 61.5
    Private collection

83 To the Studios 1985
    oil on canvas
    52¼ × 52¼, 132.7 × 132.7
    Marlborough Fine Art, London

84 From the Studios 1987
    oil on canvas
    52¼ × 48⅜, 132.7 × 122.9
    Private collection

85 Head of J.Y.M. IV 1986
    oil on canvas
    20⅛ × 16⅛, 51.1 × 40.9
    Private collection

86 J.Y.M. Seated 1986–87
    oil on canvas
    28 × 26, 71.1 × 66
    Saatchi Collection, London

87 Head of Catherine Lampert 1986
    oil on canvas
    20¼ × 18½, 51.4 × 47
    Private collection

88 Head of David Landau 1987
oil on canvas
$26\frac{5}{8} \times 24\frac{1}{2}$, 67.6 × 62.2
Private collection

89 Julia 1987
Acrylic on board
18 × 16, 45.7 × 40.6
Marlborough Fine Art, London

90 J.Y.M. Seated 1987–88
oil on canvas
$21\frac{1}{2} \times 18$, 54.6 × 45.7
Private collection

91 Portrait of Catherine Lampert 1987
oil on canvas
26 × 24, 66 × 61
Private collection, New York

92 The Chimney – Mornington Crescent II 1988
oil on canvas
$60\frac{1}{4} \times 52\frac{1}{8}$, 153 × 132.4
Private collection

93 Mornington Crescent – Night 1988–89
oil on canvas
$54\frac{1}{4} \times 44\frac{1}{4}$, 137.8 × 112.4
Private collection, Switzerland

94 E.O.W. Nude 1954
oil on canvas
14 × 18, 35.5 × 45.7
Private collection

95 Half-Length Nude 1958
oil on board
24 × 20, 61 × 50.8
Jonathan Roemer

96 Head of E.O.W. 1955
oil on board
31 × 26, 78.7 × 66
University of Cincinnati

97 Head of E.O.W. 1956
charcoal on paper
30 × 22, 76.2 × 55.9
Ruth Roemer

98 Head of E.O.W. 1956
charcoal on paper
30 × 22, 76.2 × 55.9
signed and dated upper left
Private collection

99 Head of E.O.W. 1957
charcoal on paper
30 × 22, 76.2 × 55.9
dated upper left
David Roemer

100 Head of Leon Kossoff 1957
charcoal on paper
30 × 22, 76.2 × 55.9
signed and dated upper left and right
Private collection

101 Head of E.O.W. 1960
charcoal on paper
$30\frac{3}{4} \times 22\frac{3}{4}$, 78.1 × 57.7
Whitworth Art Gallery, University of Manchester

102 Head of E.O.W. I 1960
oil on canvas
16 × 13, 40.6 × 33
Private collection

103 Head of Julia 1960
charcoal on paper
30 × 22, 76.2 × 55.9
Private collection

104 Seated Figure II 1961
oil on board
19 × 16, 48.2 × 40.6
David Roemer

105 Head of E.O.W. 1967
oil on canvas
17 × 14, 43.2 × 35.5
Private collection

106 Head of Gerda Boehm 1961
charcoal on paper
30 × 22, 76.2 × 55.9
Private collection

107 Head of Gerda Boehm II 1961
charcoal on paper
30 × 22, 76.2 × 55.9
signed and dated upper left
Private collection

108 E.O.W., Nude on Bed 1959
oil on canvas
30 × 24, 76.2 × 61
Present whereabouts unknown

109 Shell Building Site from the Festival Hall 1959
oil on board
49 × 60, 124.5 × 152.4
Gray Art Gallery and Museum, Hartlepool

110 Shell Building Site from the Thames 1959
oil on board
60 × 48, 152.4 × 121.9
Thyssen-Bornemisza Collection, Lugano, Switzerland

111 Nude on Bed III 1961
oil on canvas
18 × 24, 45.7 × 61
Private collection

112 E.O.W., Nude Lying on her Back 1959
oil on canvas
16 × 20, 40.6 × 50.8
David Roemer

113 Head of E.O.W. 1961
oil on board
$14\frac{1}{2}$ × 12, 36.8 × 30.5
Private collection

114 E.O.W. Looking into Fire II 1962
oil on canvas
18 × 16, 45.7 × 40.6
Private collection

115 Head of E.O.W. II 1964
oil on board
14 × 11, 35.5 × 28
Private collection

116 E.O.W. Head on her Pillow 1965
oil on board
$10\frac{1}{2}$ × 14, 26.7 × 35.5
Private collection

117 E.O.W. Sleeping II 1966
oil on board
$6\frac{1}{2}$ × 14, 16.7 × 35.5
Private collection

118 Head of E.O.W. 1964
oil on board
18 × 15, 45.7 × 38.1
Private collection

119 Head of Gerda Boehm 1965
oil on board
$17\frac{1}{2} \times 14\frac{1}{2}$, 44.5 × 36.8
Private collection

120 Behind Camden Town Station, Summer Evening 1966
oil on board
$44\frac{3}{8} \times 55$, 113.5 × 139.7
Private collection

121 Behind Camden Town Station, Autumn Evening 1965
oil on board
35 × 55, 89 × 139.7
Private collection, New York

122 Mornington Crescent 1967
oil on board
45 × 55, 114.3 × 139.7
Private collection

123 Mornington Crescent, with the Statue of Sickert's
Father-in-Law Cobden 1966
oil on board
$45\frac{1}{8} \times 55$, 114.5 × 139.7
Marlborough International Fine Art

124 Figure on a Bed II 1967
oil on board
$23\frac{3}{4} \times 31\frac{1}{2}$, 60.3 × 80
Private collection

125 Figure on Bed 1968
oil on canvas
16 × 16, 40.6 × 40.6
Private collection

126 E.O.W.'s Reclining Head 1969
oil on hardboard
$12\frac{1}{2} \times 11\frac{3}{4}$, 31.8 × 30
Private collection

127 E.O.W. Reclining 1970
oil on canvas
20 × 22, 50.8 × 55.9
Private collection

128 Head of Gerda Boehm 1971
oil on board
13 × 13, 33 × 33
Private collection

129 Head of E.O.W. II 1968
oil on canvas
$12 \times 9\frac{3}{4}$, 30.5 × 24.7
Private collection

130 Head of Paula Eyles 1969
oil on canvas
$27\frac{1}{2} \times 24$, 69.8 × 61
Private collection

131 Head of Renée Fedden 1970
oil on board
30 × 25, 76.2 × 63.5
Private collection

132 Primrose Hill, Winter 1961
oil on canvas
36 × 54, 91.4 × 137.2
Private collection

133 Primrose Hill 1958
oil on board
$36 \times 46\frac{1}{2}$, 91.4 × 118.1
Private collection

134 Primrose Hill, Summer Sunshine 1964
oil on board
$40\frac{3}{8} \times 59\frac{7}{8}$, 102.5 × 152
Arts Council Collection

135 Primrose Hill, Winter 1962
oil on canvas
$36\frac{1}{2} \times 46$, 92.7 × 116.8
Private collection

136 Primrose Hill, Summer 1968
oil on board
48 × 58, 121.9 × 147.3
Private collection

137 Study for Primrose Hill I
coloured crayon and charcoal
$9\frac{7}{8} \times 12$, 25.1 × 30.5
Private collection

138 Primrose Hill Study
ink on paper
$10 \times 12\frac{5}{8}$, 25.5 × 32
Private collection

139 Rimbaud II 1976–77
oil on board
42 × 42, 106.7 × 106.7
Saatchi Collection, London

140 Seated Model III 1963
oil on paper
$40\frac{1}{4} \times 27$, 102 × 68.6
Private collection

141 Seated Figure with Arms Raised 1973–74
oil on board
28 × 28, 71.1 × 71.1
Private collection

142 Seated Figure with Arms Raised 1973
oil on board
16 × 16, 40.6 × 40.6
Private collection

143 Head of J.Y.M. 1970
oil on board
14 × 14, 35.5 × 35.5
Private collection

144 Head of J.Y.M. 1972
oil on board
24 × 28, 61 × 71.1
Private collection

145 Head of E.O.W. 1972
oil on board
$13\frac{3}{8} \times 8\frac{3}{4}$, 34 × 22
Collection R. B. Kitaj

146 Head of E.O.W. 1973
oil on board
$13 \times 8\frac{1}{2}$, 33 × 21.6
Private collection

147 Head of E.O.W. 1972
oil on board
14 × 12, 35.5 × 30.5
James Kirkman, London

148 Head of Brigid 1973–74
mixed chalks on paper
$22 \times 30\frac{1}{2}$, 55.9 × 77.5
inscribed, signed and dated lower left
Arts Council Collection

149 Head of Michael Podro 1976
chalk and charcoal on paper
$30 \times 22\frac{1}{2}$, 76.2 × 57.1
Private collection

150 Head of C. D. II 1977
chalk and charcoal on paper
29 × 22, 73.7 × 55.9
dated upper left
Yale Center for British Art, Paul Mellon Collection,
New Haven

151 Head of Ken Garland 1977–78
chalk and charcoal on paper
22½ × 30¼, 57.1 × 76.8
signed and dated upper left
The British Council

152 Head of Catherine Lampert VI 1980
chalk and charcoal on paper
30⅜ × 23, 77.2 × 58.4
dated upper left
Museum of Modern Art, New York

153 J.Y.M. Seated III 1981
chalk and charcoal on paper
30⅜ × 22¾, 77.2 × 57.7
signed and dated lower left
Bolton Museum and Art Gallery

154 Head of Margaret Schuelein 1983
chalk and charcoal on paper
29 × 22, 73.7 × 55.9
signed and dated lower left
Private collection

155 Head of J.Y.M. 1984
charcoal on paper
31 × 28, 78.7 × 71.1
signed and dated lower left
Private collection

156 Head of J.Y.M. 1986
charcoal on paper
34¼ × 30¼, 87 × 76.8
signed and dated lower left
Private collection

157 Head of Catherine Lampert 1985–86
charcoal and chalk on paper
30½ × 29½, 77.5 × 75
signed and dated lower right
Private collection

158 Head of Julia II 1986
charcoal on paper
30¼ × 34½, 76.8 × 87.6
signed and dated lower left
Private collection

159 Head of Julia 1989
chalk and charcoal on paper
38¼ × 29¾, 97.2 × 75.5
signed and dated lower left
Private collection

160 J.Y.M. 1988–89
chalk, charcoal and indian ink on paper
32¾ × 36, 83.2 × 91.4
signed and dated lower left
Susan Kasen Summer and Robert Summer

161 Head of Gerda Boehm II 1978–79
chalk and charcoal on paper
30½ × 22⅜, 77.5 × 57.5
signed and dated lower right
Private collection

162 Head of Gerda Boehm 1978–79
oil on board
22¼ × 28, 56.5 × 71.1
Private collection

163 Portrait of Sandra 1973–74
mixed chalks on paper
32 × 22, 81.3 × 55.9
signed and dated lower left
Collection R. B. Kitaj

164–203 Work in progress for Portrait of Sandra 1973–74
40 photographs, the last of the final work (*see* 163)
Photo Sandra Fisher

204 J.Y.M. Seated IV 1979
oil on board
22 × 18, 55.9 × 45.7
Private collection

205 Head of J.Y.M. 1973–74
oil on board
24 × 28, 61 × 71.1
Private collection

206 Head of J.Y.M. 1974
oil on board
28 × 24, 71.1 × 61
Private collection

207 Reclining Head of J.Y.M. 1974–75
oil on board
13 × 11, 33 × 28
Private collection

208 Reclining Head of J.Y.M. 1975
oil on board
28 × 24, 71.1 × 61
Private collection

209 Portrait of J.Y.M. Seated 1976
oil on board
16 × 13, 40.6 × 33
Private collection

210 Head of J.Y.M. III 1985
oil on canvas
17 × 14, 43.2 × 35.5
Private collection

211 Head of J.Y.M. – Profile IV 1987
oil on canvas
20 × 22, 50.8 × 55.9
Marlborough International Fine Art

212 Head of J.Y.M. III 1980
oil on board
28 × 24, 71.1 × 61
The British Council

213 Head of Charlotte Podro 1982
oil on paper
30 × 22½, 76.2 × 57.1
Private collection

214 Portrait of Debbie Ratcliff 1983–84
oil on canvas
18 × 16, 45.7 × 40.6
Private collection

215 Portrait of Debbie Ratcliff III 1984
oil on canvas
26 × 26, 66 × 66
Private collection

216 Head of Catherine Lampert 1984–85
oil on canvas
26 × 24, 66 × 61
Private collection

217 Head of Julia II 1985
oil on canvas
18 × 16⅛, 45.7 × 40.9
Private collection

218 Head of David Landau 1988–89
     oil on canvas
     26⅜ × 28, 66.5 × 71.1
     Private collection

219 Summer – Tretire 1975
     chalk and charcoal on paper
     30 × 29½, 76.2 × 75
     Private collection

220 Tree at Tretire 1975
     chalk and charcoal on paper
     28½ × 30½, 72.4 × 77.5
     Private collection

221 Primrose Hill 1980
     oil on board
     58 × 48, 147.3 × 121.9
     Private collection

222 Primrose Hill Study – Autumn Evening 1979
     oil on board
     20 × 16¼, 50.8 × 41.3
     Private collection

223 Euston Steps – Study 1980–81
     oil on board
     48 × 60, 121.9 × 152.4
     Arts Council Collection

224–25 Two pages of sketches for To the Studios 1985
         mixed media

226 To the Studios 1985
     (see 83)

227 Mornington Crescent – Early Morning 1989–90
     oil on canvas
     20¼ × 16¼, 51.4 × 41.3
     Marlborough Fine Art, London

228 Chimney in Mornington Crescent – Early Morning
     1988–89
     oil on canvas
     54⅛ × 44⅛, 137.5 × 112.1
     Private collection

Comparative Illustrations

Page 89
Sickert *Nuit d'Eté c.* 1906
oil on canvas
20 × 16, 50.8 × 40.6
Private collection, London

Sickert *L'Affaire de Camden Town* 1909
oil on canvas
24 × 16, 61 × 40.6
Private collection

Page 149
Matisse *Pink Nude* 1935 (work in progress)
Four of twenty-two photographs, states I,
IX, XIII and the final work:
oil on canvas
26 × 36½, 66 × 92.7
Baltimore Museum of Art, Cone Collection

de Kooning *Woman I* 1950–52
oil on canvas
75⅞ × 58, 192.4 × 147.6
The Museum of Modern Art, New York

Rembrandt *The Deposition* or
Lamentation over the Dead Christ 1637–38 and early 1640s
grisaille, oil on paper on canvas on oak
$12\frac{7}{8} \times 10\frac{1}{2}$, 31.9 × 26.7
National Gallery, London

Page 158
Hogarth *The Shrimp Girl* after 1740
oil on canvas
25 × 20, 63.5 × 50.8
National Gallery, London

Manet *Berthe Morisot with a Bunch of Violets* 1872
oil on canvas
$21\frac{5}{8} \times 15$, 55 × 38
Private collection

Page 159
Rodin *Iris* c. 1890–91
bronze
$32\frac{7}{8} \times 31\frac{3}{4} \times 16$, 83.5 × 80.5 × 40.5
Private collection

Page 163
de Stael *Composition* 1950
oil on canvas
24 × 33, 61 × 83.8
Private collection

Page 166
Bacon *Study for Portrait of Henrietta Moraes on Red Ground* 1964
oil on canvas
78 × 57, 198 × 145
Private collection

Page 168
Goya *The Pilgrimage to San Isidro* 1820–23 (detail)
oil on canvas
$55\frac{1}{8} \times 172\frac{3}{8}$, 140 × 438
Museo del Prado, Madrid

Page 170
Constable *Salisbury Cathedral from the Meadows* 1831
oil on canvas
$59\frac{3}{4} \times 74\frac{3}{4}$, 151.8 × 189.9
Loan to the National Gallery, London

Rembrandt *The Three Trees* 1643
etching with drypoint
$8\frac{3}{8} \times 11$, 21.3 × 27.9
British Museum, London

Rubens *Autumn Landscape with View of Het Steen in the Early Morning* 1636
oil on canvas
$51\frac{5}{8} \times 90\frac{1}{4}$, 131.1 × 229.2
National Gallery, London

Constable *Hadleigh Castle* 1829
oil on canvas
$48 \times 64\frac{3}{4}$, 122 × 164.5
Yale Center for British Art, Paul Mellon Collection,
New Haven

Page 171
Philips Koninck *Road by a Ruin* 1655
oil on canvas
$54\frac{1}{8} \times 66$, 137.4 × 167.7
National Gallery, London

Bomberg *Jerusalem, looking to Mount Scopus* 1925
oil on canvas
$22\frac{1}{4} \times 29\frac{5}{8}$, 56.5 × 75.2
Tate Gallery, London

Page 174
Studio of Titian *Tarquin and Lucretia* c. 1570 (unfinished)
oil on canvas
Gemäldegalerie der Akademie der bildenden Künste, Vienna

Page 175
Titian *Bacchus and Ariadne* 1522–23
oil on canvas
69 × 75, 175.2 × 190.5
National Gallery, London

Page 177
Rimbaud at 17, from the cover of *Illuminations*. Photo Carjat

Bernini *Ecstasy of St Teresa* 1645–52, in the Cornaro Chapel,
St Maria della Vittoria, Rome. Detail of an eighteenth-century
painting in the Schwerin Museum. Photo A. Heuschkel

Page 179
Velázquez *Sebastián de Morra* (the dwarf) 1644
oil on canvas
41⅝ × 31⅞, 106 × 81
Museo del Prado, Madrid

Page 205
Rembrandt *Portrait of Hendrickje Stoffels* 1659
oil on canvas
40¼ × 33¾, 101.9 × 83.7
National Gallery, London

Page 212
Courbet *The Oak of Vercingetorix* or *The Oak at Flagey* 1864
oil on canvas
35 × 43⅜, 89 × 110
Murauchi Art Museum, Tokyo

Photographs

Frontispiece Frank Auerbach in his studio, 1989.
Photo Julia Auerbach

Page 220
Auerbach's studio, 1985
© The Artist. Photo Prudence Cuming Associates